The E

Advocating for Your Deaf or Hard of Hearing Child

Edited by Sara Kennedy and Karen Putz

HANDS&
VOICES™

Hands & Voices
PO Box 3093
Boulder CO 80307
(303) 492-6283
parentadvocate@handsandvoices.org
www.handsandvoices.org

We receive many requests for educational advocacy support at Hands & Voices, an international nonprofit with Chapters across more than forty states that has been serving families raising children who are deaf/hard of hearing including other considerations since 1996. This book is intended as a compliment to the resources available through the Advocacy Support and Training program (ASTra) to help parents sharpen their own advocacy skills through learning

ADVOCACY SUPPORT & TRAINING™

from other parents' stories, including insights from Deaf/hard of hearing adults.

Some products parents and professionals may find helpful:

Educational Advocacy for Students Who are Deaf or Hard of Hearing, by Cheryl DeConde Johnson, EdD, Leanne Seaver, MA, and Janet DesGeorges. The Guidebook is an essential tool for families, advocates and professionals and covers special education and civil rights laws, the parts of the IEP or 504 Plan, and strategies for access and meaningful educational progress and inclusion.

Advocacy 101: A video about learning to be your child's best advocate.

The I.E.P. Meeting Planner: Set your child up for success by planning ahead.

ASTra Training: Introductory and advanced educational advocacy training is available through Hands & Voices Chapters only. Contact astra@handsandvoices.org for more information.

See these and more resources on the Hands & Voices website at https://handsandvoices.org/astra/index.html

Foreword

by Djenne Amal-Morris

We have been at that IEP meeting where our child's needs and strengths did not seem to relate to the cookie-cutter plan proposed.

Many of us have experienced an IEP meeting where our child's strengths and educational needs exceeded the proposed plan given by professionals. We may even have had our child's eligibility or abilities questioned. We understand what it is like to be seen as "just the parent" in a sea of administrators.

And we have celebrated with a team who saw our unique child's gifts and used them to bridge the gaps in academic or social skills.

This book is for you, the parent who finds themselves reading late at night about IDEA law, how this works on "special needs" parent websites, and worrying through their child's next IEP. If you are an administrator, educator, therapist, audiologist, advocate or other professional, this book will help you understand the passion behind parent advocacy and how best to partner with families.

We hope this is a breath of fresh air both in content (what can you ask for?) and spirit (parents voices do matter!).

Contents

Note: *This book is written by parents who are "there and doing it", who have learned the laws, are perfecting their advocacy skills, and who are determined to ensure their child and every child is receiving the best education possible.*

Throughout the book, each family identifies with different terminology. You may see Deaf, deaf, hard of hearing, Deaf/Hard of hearing Plus or other terms such as "hearing loss" or "hearing differences". We chose to let each author define and speak for themselves in their own words.

*Always go with your initial instinct
when you think your child isn't getting
the help they need, and don't be
intimidated by people who think they
know better or have more professional
experience. You know your child best.*

- Elizabeth Greeno

Introduction: Advocacy Begins Early

By Sara Kennedy

As a parent of a child who is deaf/hard of hearing, you may have heard stories by now about how you must become your child's strongest advocate. Community systems and schools are often not prepared to accommodate our kids with any "low-incidence" condition: hearing differences are one of those. They might have additional complex needs as well. How and where do you begin to learn everything you will need to know? This scared me early on, and there was a big learning curve.

The love for and the primal need to protect your child can overcome your fear of the unknown ahead. As you are beginning to move past processing the news about your child's hearing difference, you realize there is much to learn about seeing the world through your child's perspective. How does your child experience the world? Knowledgeable audiologists, teachers, early interventionists, other parents and deaf/hard of hearing adults will inform your journey, but each parent puts in the hard work to see the world as their own child does. We must learn the concepts and terms we need to know and the rules the new systems play by, whether in early intervention for our youngest kids, or insurance, education, special education, 504 Plans, or community access for our young adult. While there is much on the internet, often that firehose of information lacks significant wisdom specific to our own child's unique needs. Proceed with caution. Better to develop relationships with trusted people who know your child firsthand and a few trusted websites as your knowledge grows.

Start with a vision of the graduate in the cradle. Building up a child's self-confidence starts with how they see themselves in your eyes. Your child drinks in your response and expression when others wonder out loud, "What are those things in his ears?" or "Why are you moving your hands like that for a baby?" Your child takes to heart how you deal with a school photographer wanting to take off hearing aids for the school picture (what does that action tell a child?) or other children asking their innocent but pointed questions. (My favorite: "I bet your baby could hear better if you took those things out of her ears. I can't hear when my mom makes me wear those things at the pool.") If you can hold any feelings of insecurity or doubt at bay while responding decisively and with good humor that your baby is, in fact, just fine, you are a step ahead. "Well, Aunt Amy, we actually think this is a great time to be deaf/hard of hearing. There are captions, images are primary, everyone texts or messages instead of using the phone, hearing technology is better than ever, and sign language (or cued language), or whatever supports you are using is cooler than ever. Anyway, our baby is doing great and we are learning so much about language and meeting terrific people!" Craft your own message of how great your child is and let your child "catch" you sharing your good feelings about their gifts often. When you introduce your child, lead with personality, not hearing level.

Self-Advocacy: What is it?

One definition stands out in the literature: "The realization of strengths and weaknesses, the ability to formulate personal goals, being assertive, and making decisions." (Martin, J., et al., 1993) What a powerful concept! What parent doesn't hope and work towards the outcome when their child will be able to:

- Describe his/her own skills and needs
- Set life goals and create a plan to reach them
- Know the how, who, and when to ask for help when needed
- Make decisions and take responsibility for consequences
- Understand the laws that cover the right to equal access and how to use them
- Create their own community of friends, support, and meaning?

Looking at your young child, how do you begin the road to get to that final goal of raising a strong self-advocate? Little by little. Help them develop the skills to know when their "sound" is working, when they can't see the interpreter well when they need a little less background noise to function. Let them face some consequences of their decisions to develop more thinking skills. (Yes, occasionally I said I couldn't get batteries to school.) We want to develop a growth mindset "I am not good at this...yet!" instead of a learned helplessness stance when faced with a challenge.

Children need lots of practice in making decisions. They can't learn that if we are always "fixing" situations for them behind the scenes. If parents share their thinking process as toddlers grow into middle schoolers, they benefit greatly! Adults can share real-life problems: "We scheduled your birthday party on the same day as the soccer tournament!" Work through them together or at least share your problem-solving process, giving a child a chance to learn important concepts. A child will learn that people make mistakes and then how to recover, what is a fact versus opinion, and that people change their minds or have "big feelings" just like they experience.

The idea of "narrating your day" (note that this can be signed, spoken, cued, or more than one of these) for young children enriches their brain capacity and understanding. Narrating is not supposed to be a long passive litany, but many opportunities to give and take (serve and return, if you will) in conversation during the day. If we see our child looking curious or afraid, we can name that feeling that we see and respond to it. They need to learn the terms for thinking and feeling (worry, idea, dream, frustrated, satisfied, suspicious) as part of their own future safety and independence. On average, our kids develop this skill of being able to "think about thinking" later than hearing kids. (https://publications.aap.org/pediatrics/article/146/Supplement_3/S231/34525/Pragmatics-in-Deaf-and-Hard-of-Hearing-Children-An. One area of particular emphasis should be the ability to retell a story with a beginning, middle, and end that is clear to the listener. (Look up the Theory of Mind and pragmatic language (social language) to learn more.)

The dividing line between eligibility for an IEP and for placement on a 504 Plan is the need for specialized instruction and related services At some point, an educational team may mention that your child may no longer be eligible for an IEP if they are doing well academically.

Experienced advocates will tell you this: If your child can explain and advocate for their learning, access and equipment needs to current teachers, future employers, professors and roommates, effectively meet and work with a new physician, department of motor vehicles staff, bankers, co-workers, potential friends and partners, and troubleshoot equipment and mastermind communication repair among diverse groups of people without assistance, understanding their rights under the IDEA and or ADA laws, and navigating their transition from high school without support, they may be ready to leave the structure of the IEP. And not a moment beforehand. Why remove supports that have contributed to a child's success prematurely, and often long before transition from high school needs are even assessed?

Planning for Positive Childhood Experiences

This community of parents dug into "what works" and learned about the key actions of parents that can make a difference for a child's future. Teaching them to be as self-sufficient as possible---from life skills to relationship skills-- early on is key. Prompt their self-advocacy through modeling and asking "does this work for you?". Celebrate those times when your child does advocate for themselves, or even begins to approximate that lifelong skill. Keeping our expectations high while watching for barriers to access, needed supports, and keeping our eyes on the whole child is critical. We can't do anything now about how early our child was identified or their level of hearing once identified, but we can impact these seven areas of positive childhood experiences. We can work to improve each one of these. The more of these experiences a child has, the greater the buffer against any adversity they may face growing up. (https://avahealth.org/aces/positive-childhood-experiences.html)

Consider this a to-do list for fostering joy and positive relationships at your house.

Positive Childhood Experiences

1. Ability to talk about feelings with family members
2. Finds family member(s) supportive in difficult times

3. Enjoys participation in community traditions (including family traditions)

4. Feeling of belonging in high school (start early with that in mind!)

5. Feeling of being supported by friends (particularly in high school)

6. Having at least two non-parent adults who genuinely care. Build up your child's network with other adults.

7. Feeling safe and protected by an adult at home. One caring adult can truly make a difference

With this foundation, you will be fostering self-confidence and self-advocacy skills from the very start in a world that is not always welcoming of differences.

"

In special education, there's too much emphasis placed on the deficit and not enough on the strength.

- Temple Grandin

Finding Your Vision as an Advocate

By Rosabel O. Agbayani, MPH

Sometimes we think that in order to make change we have to make a lot of noise. What I have learned from raising my children, and especially raising my deaf child, is that you have to be able to drown out the noise and listen to your heart.

I'm not sure why I was so shocked to learn that my son was deaf, because the news came after almost six months of testing. We finally had an answer. I still remember that feeling when I heard the words: "Your son has a hearing loss." My heart sank, tears fell, and an overwhelming feeling of shock took over. While the audiologist had many well-meaning things to say, it didn't reach me. I felt like I was in the scene of a Charlie Brown cartoon where the adults talked gibberish. All I could focus on was "What was my son's life going to be like?" "What is our family's life going to be like?"

Coming home from that appointment, I felt defeated. But with a six-month old infant, a teenager, and now a Deaf child, I had no time to feel sorry for myself. I spent a lot of time on the internet looking to find answers to calm the worries in my head. We asked for second opinions and I went through parent training modules, but there was no place on the internet that reassured me that everything was going to be okay.

As loving and caring as my husband is, his priority was making sure we had food on the table and a roof over our head, especially then, as owners of a small family business. Finding out our son was deaf in the midst of an economic downturn meant we were both working hard. There was some risk of losing our business and our home all at the same time. I couldn't expect him to be there for me emotionally when he was working so hard to take care of our family. Reaching out to extended family had challenges of its own. Those closest to me felt pity for our circumstance. Pity was not going to help me, so I found myself getting angry with them and frustrated having to explain what I was trying to do for my child. To further complicate the issue, in my culture and within the community of family, disabilities are not something to be discussed. There is almost a sense of pride involved. Filipinos have a tendency not to share, for fear that if others realize our weakness, then we, ourselves, are perceived as weak and therefore bring shame to a family. So even in my own family, I felt lost and out of place while going through a grieving process. I kept a lot of feelings to myself. I had no choice but to be strong, which was a constant struggle and often a lonely process.

In fact, we lost a lot of friends and family along the way. Well-meaning individuals who would minimize his hearing loss, or say things like "Well, just get a set of Rosetta Stone tapes and he will learn language like normal." One of the most hurtful things I witnessed was at a family party when my nephews were playing a game of "Can you hear me now?" They would walk around my son asking him if he could hear them. Because my son is the playful type, he innocently went along with the game while they laughed at his expense. It was then that I realized the true meaning of "You must learn to walk away from the things that no longer serve you." It was a painful but necessary lesson. Their noise was clouding my vision.

At the time when my son was diagnosed, I only knew three people who were Deaf. My uncle (my mother's youngest brother) who had been deaf since he was an infant, an uncle who became deaf as an adult, and a friend I met later in life. I asked so many questions about what their lives were like, what challenges they had to overcome and how they got to be who they were today. Deaf adults have a significant role in our understanding as parents. They have insight into the Deaf experience that is critical for my own understanding and something I can't share with my child alone.

We began to find our way, but it was not easy.

Because my son was diagnosed at the age of three, we felt great pressure to get him ready for kindergarten in a hurry. As first-time parents in the special education system, we went along with what the IEP team recommended. We were told since he "only" had a mild/moderate hearing loss that placement in a "Deaf" program was not necessary. Instead, he was placed in a noncategorical "special day class" with children who had all types of special education needs. . Within the first two weeks in this classroom, we knew that this placement was not right for him. My mild-mannered, happy child became easily angered and frustrated. As naive as I was to the IEP process, I knew I had to take action. I called our Program Specialist and asked for him to be placed in a classroom with students with similar needs. To my surprise we were told that our son's hearing loss was "not as severe as the other students in the class." To satisfy our curiosity, my husband and I decided to see for ourselves what the school was like. We visited a private preschool option, and to our amazement, saw how successful the students in that class were. These preschool children mirrored my own child's needs, and they were thriving in this school environment. They had language opportunities through-out the day and access to a teacher who was specifically trained to educate deaf children. I was convinced this was the right placement and determined to make sure that my child had the same opportunity. I couldn't envision any other way that he would have a chance at kindergarten readiness with his delayed identification. It took some research, many sleepless nights searching through IDEA laws, Deaf Rights, and Special Education websites, and finally finding the justification I needed to prove that my child belonged in a school with children like him, in a language-rich environment that was conducive for a deaf child to learn how to communicate. It was one of the hardest but most gratifying fights I have ever had as a mother. To this day, I am proud to say that I fought and won our first battle to get our son into the only non-public oral deaf school in our community.

Following that victory was the first time I ever felt "normal" again since his identification. I remember clearly when I walked him through the gates on the first day at his new school. We were all welcomed and greeted by mothers who were so excited to see another child admitted to the program. There were only six children at the time, with my son making the 7th student at the school. I finally felt at home with our new community. When our kids were busy learning, the parents (we proudly referred to ourselves as the "Parking Lot Moms") would gather at the local coffee shop and share our stories, retell how our children were identified, explain how they got to the school, and their journey so far. With each story I heard, my heart felt at ease. Meeting another parent who understood me without explanation was exactly the support I needed. I didn't have to speak, but just listen. Every word healed my soul. Every family who came into the school was greeted with the same hospitality and welcomed into our community. To this day, these mothers are like my sisters and our children are like siblings from another mother.

I realized how important it was to have this kind of network when you are going through something unique and unfamiliar to you. Parents can benefit when we learn from each other, when we can listen and share the choices we have made with each other. We also learn from Deaf/hard of hearing adults and the choices that shaped them, and the choices they made for themselves. We learn to open our minds to new ways to help shape our children's future. Deaf/hard of hearing adults can give us insight on the opportunities and struggles they have had, and the doors we need to help open. I am always inspired hearing stories of adults who grew up Deaf/hard of hearing. In listening to them, I can imagine my own son, and the story he will have to tell someday.

As a parent of a child with special needs, you go through many cycles of joy, pain, confusion, and brief moments of clarity. Some days you just lose it, it comes with the territory. It doesn't have to be anything significant that happens but some days are just tough.

I remember one day; it was just like most days. I was carrying my twelve-month old in my arms, dropped off my eldest at high school, and went to the hospital for one of my son's many appointments. I must have been exhausted because after one of my son's back-to-back appointments I just sat in my car and cried. The emotions I held in my heart just suddenly overwhelmed me. Beaten and broken, I wanted my faith to show me a sign, anything to help me understand why life had to be so hard. I was never angry that my son was deaf but I was frustrated because I didn't know if what I was doing was ever going to be enough.

Suddenly, my three-year-old deaf son (who had just learned how to put 2-3 words together, and I had learned what a mean length utterance was (MLU), looked at me, wiped the tears from my eyes, and said "Mom, why cry?" His sentiments made me smile. I just gave him a big hug. It was what I needed at just the right time. From that moment on I knew there was NOTHING wrong with him. He didn't know any differently that he was different. My answer was there beside me, telling me that I was doing EVERYTHING right. In his beautiful world, all he cared about was that I loved him. I was the one who was broken and HE was the one who fixed me!

I knew that if he was going to meet his goals, as a part of his IEP team, we needed to work together. I needed positive relationships with his team. After he returned to our home school, I decided to take a job as an aide in a Special Education classroom. I worked my way up to becoming a behavior Intervention Instructional Assistant working with kids on the Autism Spectrum. I also volunteered at the local Children's Hospital working with kids who were Deaf and Hard of Hearing. I also volunteered briefly for an Audiology office observing Aural Habilitation techniques used for kids with Hearing aids and Cochlear Implants.

My work experiences helped me have a different perspective beyond being my son's mom. I came to understand their role better, and how it does not take away from the real learning that comes from home. Professionals and educators hold the piece of the puzzle. It's our job as parents to put the pieces together in a way that fits best for our family.

As a parent and a "wannabe" professional, I met auditory verbal therapists, ENTs, speech pathologists, occupational therapists, reading specialists, Deaf educators, and specialists along the way who gave me different tools to use. I like to think of these moments like a trip to the "Special Needs Home Depot". You can fill your toolbox with many tools and use it if (and when) the time is right. I filled my head with a lot of information, gave myself the opportunity to fill my toolbox as much as I could. I didn't want to miss the opportunity of having something fit just right for my family or for the children that I worked with. My advice for new families is to always keep that toolbox open and learn as much as you can. Together with your child you can figure out what works best.

A New "Together"

Togetherness is a concept that speaks to the core of what it was like for me parenting a child who is D/HH. It is a recurring theme in my life, in our journey as a family, and now for me as a professional. When everything was falling apart, I struggled to keep my heart, my family, and my community together. Some days were better than others and progress was not always perfect or prompt. What gave me hope when times were tough was realizing that along the road, I walked the journey with people (my son, my·family, D/HH parents, and everyone else that crossed my path) who reminded me that I was not alone.

Together we grow. While my son was learning how to speak, learn, read, write, communicate- I was learning too! When he struggled, I learned how to help him succeed. While his knowledge of the world around him grew into his identity, his identity helped define who I am today. His deafness helped me learn how to listen to my heart and my heart allowed me to follow my passion.

Healing begins when you can find purpose in your pain. What started off as a desperate mom looking for answers has led me on a path where I have combined my real-life experiences as a D/HH mom with the knowledge of as a professional. Because of this, I feel a responsibility to share my unique insight with others. Everyone has an important role to play. As parents, Deaf children, Deaf adults, medical professionals, educators, researchers, and advocates we all have the power to create a community for D/HH Children and their families...TOGETHER.

Be flexible, follow your child.

What works this minute, day, month or year can and very well will change, and that's okay!

Cora Shahid

Advocacy Tips for Systems Change

By Laura Obara Gramer

I am a parent who is deaf and advocating to improve programs and services for deaf/hard of hearing students in the Pacific Northwest. I am deep in this advocacy work because my two children are deaf and I want my children and their deaf/hard of hearing peers to have access to education.

Right now, my barrier with the school district is at the district/leadership level. Other parents and I have been working hard at the school level to make the program more inclusive and more Deaf/hard of hearing (D/HH) friendly. However, we still run into barriers from the district level. I have been in the trenches for almost six years.

Here are my tips for making change:

Always remember **why** you are advocating for change. My goal was to improve access to education for all D/HH students- not just my children.

Include **all** stakeholders, including people who may have different education approaches toward D/HH education than your own philosophies. Be willing to listen and find common ground. This approach means inviting them to the table and have them share their stories/concerns.

Have thick skin because you will meet parents (and others) who will tear you down. In my case, I am a deaf person who also happens to be a parent. One parent told me and the working committee that her child will never be like me or other D/HH people.

Also **be prepared** to stand your ground with professionals who do not understand D/HH education because they have been trained in general disabilities and do not necessarily understand the nuances of D/HH education. Sadly, there are some professionals who are biased due to their training and may not be open to other methods.

Document this and ask for changes in staff training and services on your child's IEP/504 team or advocate for access in school.

Do invite the D/HH community in your efforts to change a system. They are powerful allies. Tell them what you are trying to change and who is involved. Consider reaching out to state agencies that support D/HH communities. Remind everyone what the goal is.

There will be moments where you will feel like you are finished and ready to abandon ship. There will be times you will be mad. It's okay to feel that way. Take a break, take care of yourself, remember the "why" and get back into it.

Do remember all the small changes you and the other parents have influenced (either at the district or school level), such as morning announcements in ASL, movie nights at school are always captioned (whether if a D/HH person is there or not), your child's hearing peer made their party accessible for your child, etc.)

Changing a system is a **long game**. Sometimes, we get lucky and things start changing immediately. Sometimes, things take longer especially when you are trying to change things at the system level. There could be a change of leadership (which you may have to educate the new leadership), the process the district may need to go through (legally or not), and other roadblocks that can impede progress.

Throughout all this, remember to stay calm, be prepared to speak, listen to others, and keep moving forward toward your goal.

"

Ross Greene, Ph.D., (Lives in the Balance) says "kids do well if they can." Have we given them the access, the tools, and the support they need? Do we give them opportunities to truly grow?

Sara Kennedy

Where to Begin: Build Relationships

By Andrea Marwah

"I'm going to get what my child needs no matter the cost."

Ever feel or say a statement like this? Ever feel so frustrated with your school district that you're ready to scream? I'm sure we all have. Even those of us who appear to have seamless IEPs and workable teams may feel this way from time to time. What we should consider, however, is the ramifications of this and similar "Let's go to war" statements. What is the actual cost of being a very forceful parent?

An IEP team needs to be open-minded, flexible and respectful. They should be knowledgeable, certainly. How do we build these relationships with school personnel and how will it mold our child's journey through school? We all know the saying "the squeaky wheel gets the grease." This is true, right? But we should also consider that after a while the squeaky wheel just goes unnoticed and becomes more and more "damaged." The same goes for your relationship with a school. Once that relationship is damaged, it takes many years to repair. Some relationships may not be salvageable. So, what can we do to make sure we do NOT damage the ever-necessary parent/school relationship?

Many things come to mind but first and foremost we need to behave. It's easy to get angry and blow up in the face of adversity. The problem isn't during the act of "blowing up." The problem is that many professionals discount the highly emotional or angry parent. We can easily go in and throw an "adult" temper tantrum to get what we want but then every time thereafter we will have to fight harder for what we need for our child. We also need to remember that our children are watching us. Our main goal of successful advocacy is to teach our children how to stand up for their own needs. We wouldn't want them going into the classroom and start squeaking about what they need, would we? We want to model more reasoned, respectful, collaborative actions.

So, here are a few steps to consider in maintaining a healthy parent/school relationship:

1. Work with your team, if you wish to be considered a respected team member, you need to respect the other members. This doesn't mean you have to always agree with what is said, but it does mean one should show respect for expertise.

2. Always be prepared for any school meeting or conversation. The more prepared you are the more your team will in fact accept you as a knowledgeable team participant.

3. Always cool off before speaking with school personnel. Don't immediately go in with both guns blazing; it's more effective to have your well thought out rationale ready.

4. Don't lose your cool. There is nothing more detrimental than the impact of an adult temper tantrum. Screaming, demeaning and demanding are never a good idea.

5. Find ways that you can turn a negative situation into a positive one. Come to meetings or conversations with ideas that work. Sometimes school personnel may just be stumped as to what to do or need a parent to bring up a need in the program.

6. Consider ways to create positive relationships with the team outside of the meeting. Don't settle for communicating just once a year. Even if you can't volunteer or support the school, you can thank a teacher or a therapist for an especially good experience or troubleshooting for your child.

The law names parents as equal members of the IEP team. Reaching decisions in an IEP meeting is a group process. The law doesn't name parents as the leaders, but it is clear we should be equal participants. How we come prepared to problem-solve at the meeting shows us as the experts on our own children. The others around the table are experts in their specialty. Allow them their expertise, disagree in a respectful way and I would bet your team meeting will be more successful and your child will benefit. Don't be that parent that the school dreads to see coming through the front door. It may work once but you will end up working harder and longer for everything your child needs from that point forward. Be a good model for your child. It is possible to have a productive, even happy, IEP meeting.

I was overwhelmed with close to 25 people in the room. I could not keep straight what each person's title was, let alone how to understand each page of the IEP.

I tried to give input, but my input was "mother-style", not given to fit how I now understand the law and my daughter's rights. I didn't comprehend at the time that my input was equal to the importance of the other IEP team members.

Laurie Pachl

Placement: Not Deaf Enough

By Theresia M. Carrigan

My daughter was identified as hard of hearing at age five. She has other disabilities that took our attention in her first years, and it was not until we had an in-depth speech-language evaluation that led us to an audiology exam that we learned she had a moderate loss in her left ear and a mild loss in her right. I was not upset about this, as I am hard of hearing myself, but I was suddenly sitting up and taking notice of what additional steps we would need to take to have her needs met by her school. At first our school wanted to treat this like it was not a big deal, and refused any services in American Sign Language (ASL). They continued to do so throughout that first school year.

About a month after our first IEP meeting where the school system audiologist stonewalled my desire to have ASL support, I began to investigate the state School for the Deaf. A month after that, my daughter visited the School for the Deaf twice, and they considered whether she would be a good fit for their program. I crossed my fingers and wished very hard, and after a week, they decided that my daughter could start at any time. I was ready right then to help her transition to the School for the Deaf--however, since I shared legal custody with her father, I needed to get his agreement. He, believing like the public-school personnel that she is "not Deaf enough" to need Deaf/HH services, blocked her placement, and told the School for the Deaf that if I enrolled her, he would drive to the school and disenroll her. The school decided it was better not to get in the middle of a custody battle and told me that when we had an agreement or a court order, she would be welcomed with open arms.

Then I really kicked it into high gear. I had her assessed at a local neurodevelopmental clinic which is set up specifically for Deaf and Hard of Hearing children. I hired a lawyer. I reached out to the National Association for the Deaf, to our state Governor's Office for the Deaf and Hard of Hearing, and to Parent Connections who all offered their support in getting my daughter into the environment she needed. These organizations offered advice, a sounding board, and moral support while I went through the process of fighting for access within our public school system at the same time as fighting to get her into the School for the Deaf.

While we were waiting for our court date, her father met with the public school system audiologist, who again tried to discourage a placement at the School for the Deaf, despite the School itself admitting her and the neurodevelopmental assessment indicating that she would benefit from visual language. I kept strong and rallied my friends and supporters around us. I started signing with my daughter in earnest and started an ASL club in our suburban town so she could be around other signers. I saw our circle start to grow, and I saw how strong we were.

When the day finally came for us to go to court, I was filing for full custody. I had my lawyer by my side, which my friends had helped pay for through Go-Fund-Me. My lawyer and I had obtained signed statements from a half dozen professionals who agreed that my daughter needed visual language and access to Deaf Services at the School for the Deaf—but it turns out we didn't need them. When we came before the family court magistrate, he first asked my ex-husband what evidence he had that such a placement would be detrimental to my daughter. He asked him if he had brought witnesses or statements. He had not. He had his notes from his conversation with the district audiologist, which was considered hearsay. He had no evidence.

The magistrate recommended that we come to an agreement rather than pursue a hearing: my ex-husband could maintain joint legal custody if he agreed that my daughter could attend the School for the Deaf, which the magistrate described as a "fine and well-regarded institution in our state." We agreed, and it was signed. I felt like, after months of holding my breath, I could breathe again. The next day we had a party at my house, with my hearing and Deaf friends coming together to celebrate that my daughter could access the school she needed, the school that wanted her and wanted to serve her. In the year and a half since she started at the School for the Deaf, my daughter's development in both language and academics has taken off. She is more communicative both in ASL and in English. She is thriving in the placement so many of us fought so hard for. I am so proud of her, proud of the school that we fought for, and proud of myself as her mom for acting in her best interests no matter what was thrown at me.

"

As opposed to a one-size-fits-all approach, meaningful access is a tailored fit that makes use of a variety of communication modes available to accommodate the specific needs of a deaf or hard of hearing student.

John C. Wyvill and Mari Serbrov

A Fifth Grader, His Mom, and a Lesson in Advocacy: Extracurricular Dreams

By Melanie Doyle

One of the opportunities elementary students have in our school district is to serve on Safety Patrol in the 5th grade. The police department partners with the school district to offer this program. Student participants go through extensive training to learn how to safeguard crosswalks and assist other students as they arrive and leave the school campus.

Announcements regarding the opportunity to participate in the program were made in my twin sons' fourth grade classroom. Riley, my hearing son, enthusiastically volunteered to join the Safety Patrol and go through the training program. Crosby, who has a hearing loss, heard the announcement, too. However, he had no idea what Safety Patrol was and, consequently, didn't volunteer. We drive by the Safety Patrol every morning, but this turned out to be key vocabulary that was missing from his lexicon.

By the time I was able to explain the program to Crosby and contact the coordinator, all the positions were filled. A parent volunteer who oversees the program did agree to add my son to the waiting list. Shortly after our conversation, I received an email from the school principal stating, "I received word that Crosby is interested in being on Safety Patrol. While he is on the waiting list at this point, he probably wouldn't be on the squad until the fall, so I thought it would be best to look into it now. Even after participating in two IEP meetings and reading multiple reports, I guess I still don't know enough about his hearing loss to judge his ability to hear cars, whistles and voices (all necessary) while on patrol."

Had the principal stopped there, it would have been fine. Since Crosby uses both a hearing aid and cochlear implant, it is only logical that parents would have legitimate concerns about a deaf child being

on Safety Patrol. Nonetheless, he went on to write "I was advised by the San Diego Police Department (SDPD) that an aide would need to be with him. However, since this is an optional program, the school couldn't pay for the aide. Please let me know your thoughts."

After I calmed down, (and wisely chose not to share my initial thoughts!), I responded that I appreciated his willingness to address this sensitive issue proactively. I went on to say that there are other options besides an aide that should be considered, such as a peer-buddy, FM system, or visual cues. I was concerned that having an aide by his side would counter the goal of encouraging him to become more independent. In my email response to the principal, I requested that my husband and I meet with him to explore options that would not compromise the safety of the students.

Instead of holding a meeting, he wanted to have a couple of questions answered which included asking the district's legal opinion on the matter. That's when my red flag went up! To me, this was putting the cart before the horse. The principal stated that rather than "meet multiple times due to lack of information at the outset" he wanted to wait until items that needed clarification were resolved. Conversely, I was concerned that if he did not have sufficient facts for the legal office, he would receive a faulty opinion.

Not one to sit idly by, I proceeded to call the sergeant who supervised the SDPD officer and the school district's Acting Deaf and Hard of Hearing (D/HH) Program Manager to solicit their help. I explained to them that, in my opinion, the principal and the SDPD officer had pre-determined Crosby 's capabilities without fairly assessing his ability to do the job. They had pre-determined that an aide must be present without consulting his parents, D/HH itinerant teacher, regular education teacher, classroom aide or speech therapist. Crosby had no opportunity to receive training or be objectively assessed while on the waiting list. The officer and principal were operating on the false assumption that Crosby couldn't perform the responsibilities without the support of an aide. Another word for this is prejudice; prejudging his capabilities rather than fairly assessing them. I also stated that if, after an objective assessment and training, if Crosby was not able to perform the duties of a Safety Patrol Officer, we should explore other ways to include him. Perhaps he could write down the license plate numbers of all the illegally parked cars in the crossing area, or perform some other traffic safety-related duty.

At one point along the way I had to ask myself if I was resolving this issue for me or for Crosby. I asked my son how much he wanted to be on Safety Patrol. (His answer: "A lot"). I also asked some of his service providers if I was being unrealistic to think that he could perform this function. All felt that with accommodations he would have no trouble at all. Even his twin brother gave thoughtful consideration to my question and said he could do the job.

The more confident I became that Crosby could participate in the program regardless of his severe-to-profound hearing loss, the angrier I became at the bureaucracy and run-around we were facing from both the district and the city. I started to envision headlines in the local paper reading, "Student Denied Opportunity to Participate on Safety Patrol Due to Disability." Even though I'm an active advocate for my child, I didn't have any desire to file a complaint. First of all, I wasn't clear what law would cover this issue. The Americans with Disabilities Act, Individuals with Disabilities Education Act, Section 504, and/or the California Education Code? Not that I would let this deter me--I just wasn't eager to hop on the litigation train.

I also wouldn't knowingly put my son in a position that would compromise student safety or increase the school district's liability. The other headline I imagined was, "Deaf Safety Patrol Student Contributes to Child Injured in Crosswalk." Certainly, I wouldn't want that kind of burden overshadowing my son for the rest of his life.

During this ongoing dispute, I had occasion to speak with AG Bell's Parent Section President. She helped me put this challenge into perspective by saying her child wouldn't have had this opportunity when he was growing up fifteen years ago. This made me realize that even if Crosby didn't get to participate on Safety Patrol, I had to fight this battle for all deaf and hard of hearing students. It became my responsibility to educate the police department, district administrators, parents, and students. What a great opportunity for Crosby 's peers to learn how to accommodate a student with a disability while performing a vital service to the school community. They would learn life-long skills that could carry over into their school and work environments.

After a period of inaction from both the school district and the city (they were also seeking a legal opinion from their attorney), I decided to escalate the issue and research the laws. I read the city's policy for accommodating people with disabilities, the school district's policy on student nondiscrimination and found several citations that extracurricular activities are covered in IEPs. I called the Parent Support Unit and the ombudsperson from the school district. On the city side, I contacted the lieutenant in the police department's Juvenile Services, who was compassionate and actively sought a resolution. Finally, after several phone calls, emails and meetings, it was agreed that the police department would train and assess Crosby. If an aide was needed, the school district would provide this service.

Not long after his training, we received a phone call from the San Diego Police Department informing us there was an opening on the crew. As long as the 'whistle blower' wears the FM system, Crosby was able to perform his duties. He proudly served as a full safety patrol member that fall.

Surround yourself with people who believe in your child's true potential. Reach out to D/HH adults to tap their immense wisdom.

Celebrate the joy your child brings!

Candace Lindow-Davies

A Twelve-Year Journey Advocating for Access

By Rana Ottallah

The day my daughter was born changed my life. Dalia was born via repeat C-Section and that was a blessing. She happened to be a breech baby with the umbilical cord wrapped around her neck multiple times and around her body like gift wrap; a natural birth would have been a disaster.

Dalia failed her newborn hearing screening, and I was told she most likely had fluid in her ears. We were asked to go to the hospital for a second screening. After two weeks, we did. I still remember the process. It was like pulling teeth. One ear was "good", the left ear was "referring", and finally the audiologist said all was fine and my baby girl could hear and that was the end of it, or so I thought.

When Hurricane Katrina hit the greater New Orleans area, we evacuated a couple of days before it made landfall. I was on the road with my three-month-old baby girl and my family. After hours of traveling and seeking shelter in different places, we finally settled in Alexandria, Louisiana--350 miles away from New Orleans. Our children were finally enrolled in school and we strived to return to some level of normalcy.

Months passed, and around December, I noticed Dalia was always looking at the ceiling fan and did not mind the noise that her three siblings were making. She was a "happy baby" sleeping through it all. I started to worry about her hearing. I shared my observations with my mom, but she dismissed my concerns, laughing them off.

A few days later, I mentioned my concerns to a new pediatrician, who became concerned too, and referred us to an ENT. We had to go through a couple of months of dealing with fluid in her ears, multiple rounds of antibiotics, then finally, at nine months of age, my daughter was officially diagnosed with severe to profound hearing loss. We were referred to early intervention services.

She had hearing aids fitted, which she hated. We hated the whistling sound of her hearing aids during our drive back and forth to our old home which was devastated by the hurricane. We were told to keep the hearing aids on during car rides, which was not easy, but it was based on recommendations received from different providers.

The official diagnosis with hearing loss came with so many questions and challenges. We are a Middle Eastern Arab American family. Having a daughter with a disability forced us to look at our cultural views and question if we could live within these views on disability which were not favorable.

The challenge for me as a mother was to imagine her future as an independent, self-sustaining, well-educated woman--and start planning Dalia's future with that end goal in mind. I needed to do a lot of research, I needed to educate myself on all available communication options and make sure the choice would lead to the end goal that I wanted for my child.

I wanted Dalia to be able to communicate with all family members, I did not want a barrier between her and my mother's loving, encouraging words. I wanted her to have access to her family's native language, to hear the call to prayer and the recitation of the Quran. I wanted her to experience traditional wedding ceremonies, music, songs, and traditional dance. I wanted her to be able to make friends easily and attend neighborhood schools with her siblings. I wanted to put the world in the palm of her hands and protect her from any pitiful looks and discrimination she will have to face in the future.

I made the decision to go with a cochlear implant to give her access to sound and become an oral child. That was against my ex-husband's wishes who looked at her as a beautiful baby girl without any thought of what the future struggles will bring to her.

At 13-months-old, Dalia received her first implant. We had to drive to New Orleans to the only implant center available post-Katrina. The implant was activated a few weeks later and we started the long journey of post-implant rehabilitation and teaching Dalia how to listen and how to detect sound. I was excited to watch her progress. One memorable moment was on a particularly breezy day. She actually turned to the sound of leaves moving, which was amazing to me. At two and a half years old, Dalia had a second implant. I had to find a grant to pay for that and I had to deal with a surgeon who was used to making a huge Incision to insert the implant compared to a tiny, behind the ear Incision, like her first. I cried for days at the sight of the scar, but one wise audiologist told me that a successful implant is what matters the most--and that is what we had.

First Experience with Advocacy

A few months after that, Dalia had a serious health crisis following a minor surgery that created a long-term impact which rocked her life and ours. Dalia was receiving early intervention services, but her anger and behavior after her health crises made it hard for services to continue. At that time, I was serving on my son's school PTO. I was excited to tell the principal and the speech therapist that Dalia would be attending the PK-4 class and I began explaining some of her needs. I was shocked when the principal told me "There is no place in my school for a deaf child". I remember thinking; this is a public school; she doesn't own the school and she can't dictate who can and who can't attend. This is Dalia's district school, where her brother and cousins attended, and where I wanted her to attend school.

The only thing I knew then about my child's rights were the principles of FAPE: a Free and Appropriate Public Education, and LRE, or Least Restrictive Environment. I had learned those concepts from Dalia's teacher of the deaf in early intervention. I visited the district's Deaf Education early childhood classroom housed in a different school. What they offered was not what Dalia needed. She needed oral language models, incidental learning opportunities, and peers and friends to teach her spoken words through play and spontaneous conversations.

In preschool at age three and four, we had no teacher for the deaf with early childhood certification. Instead, Dalia's services were provided by a community special education teacher with no deaf education knowledge and no way to educate Dalia's other teachers about the needs of a deaf child.

In kindergarten, the teacher had no clue about the needs of a deaf student who was oral nor how to educate and support such students. If the student did not use American Sign Language (ASL), that teacher was at a loss about how to provide support. Dalia repeated kindergarten per my request and we finally had a teacher of the deaf who changed her life.

During that time, I filed a state complaint about denying full access. I lost the argument, but turned around and filed an OCR complaint. Through negotiations, the district agreed to provide full access through a paraprofessional acting as Dalia's oral facilitator for communication.

Between second and fourth grade, things were smooth sailing. The teacher of the deaf was amazing, training the paraprofessional/oral facilitator in how to support Dalia's access and language needs. The principal was on board and allowed staff to attend training on deaf education. Louisiana amended the Deaf Child Bill of Rights, including stronger language about the rights of Deaf/hard of hearing and Deafblind students. I was one of the state advocates who pushed for that bill and pushed for other deaf rights' legislation. Tools for developing communication plans were created through a task force where I was the parent representative of a deaf oral child. I was doing lots of statewide and individual advocacy through the Louisiana Hands & Voices Chapter.

In fifth grade, things started to go downhill when Dalia transferred to a new school, the most sought-after charter school in the district. Unfortunately, they had no clue how to educate a deaf student. For the first time in years, Dalia had no services from the teacher of the deaf and had no paraprofessional/oral facilitator and had to move to a more restrictive setting to get more support. For the next two years (sixth-seventh grade), we faced a huge struggle educating staff, getting better access, dealing with personnel issues, administrative issues, and preparing and attending multiple IEP meetings each year. Finally, we decided to transfer from that school and attend the district middle school which had a lower rating, but more support.

Eighth grade started with a visit to the most amazing principal I have encountered so far. She was empathetic, understanding and was herself a mother of a child with unique needs. Dalia had full support, full access, teachers who understood her needs, administration who worked well and made an effort to get the best out of Dalia.

Who Provides Access to Technology?

All public entities, including public schools, are required under ADA to provide equal access. This is the reason why all public schools have a ramp to allow students, staff, parents and visitors who use a wheelchair to access the school building. Personally, I think "accessible" means the ability to receive the full benefit of instruction, service, entry, as any other peer. In the classroom, access means Dalia needs to be able to understand the teacher's instructions, comments, and conversations addressed to the whole class at the same level as her peers. For Deaf students who use assistive technology to access sound, this can be achieved by utilizing an FM system among other accommodations. The teacher is mandated under ADA to provide equal access to instruction to students with hearing assistive devices listed as accommodations in their IEP or 504 Plans. These devices are provided by the school district through the audiology department for the teacher to use to meet ADA access requirements.

My question and the challenge we have been facing for so many years: Why is it (often) the student's responsibility to charge the teacher's transmitter and bring it from class to class so that teachers can meet ADA requirements to accommodate the access needs of that student?

Why does the student have to be responsible for equipment used by the teacher? Who came up with this idea? Why is it considered part of the student's self-advocacy to be in charge of other's access requirements? What is done in situations with other access needs?

Dalia's self-advocacy skills she has developed from the time she attended her first IEP from age six to the present have taught her that she should not be responsible for others' access equipment. She was told she can carry the teacher's transmitter in a small pink bag. She could leave class early (missing instructional time) to get to the next class to give it early to the next teacher without her friends paying attention to that. She was told many things to try and compel her to carry the transmitter; her position never changed. She wants to be like all other students in the class. She does not want a sign over her head telling everybody she is deaf and needs accommodations. Dalia wants to get to class on time, take her time to take her books out and be prepared for class, just the same as all other students do. She wants her processor charged and ready to help her receive instructions from her teacher.

Other Deaf and hard of hearing students may hold the same position. They either choose to not use the assistive technology at all, missing valuable information, or struggle to carry it from class to class, or develop behavior to avoid using FM system.

There can be concerns about sanitation with microphones shared between multiple teachers per day or adults shadowing students going to each class in high school. I would like to see this issue of managing the transfer of the transmitter from teacher to teacher removed from the self-advocacy skill list that many teachers of the deaf are currently using to set self-advocacy goals.

With Dalia now in high school, we continue to face the constant question present at all four schools she has attended. Who provides access? What does access look like? We have had twelve years of ongoing advocacy. Every year, we have been faced with a similar challenge on this theme, and every year, we advocate for what works for Dalia.

*Decisions must be parent-driven in order
to be truly child-centered.*

Sherri Mansfield

Getting to Yes, Confessions of a Reluctant Advocate

By Christine Griffin

Even just the word "advocacy" used to make my heart beat faster, my palms sweat, and fill me with dread. This word and I are polar opposites. Even when I was a young child, if someone wanted something bad enough--be it my brother or opponents on the sports field, all anyone had to do was assert themselves and I handed over whatever they wanted. Thus, it is no wonder I felt completely inept when I had my first conversation with another parent following our children's diagnosis who said, "You are your child's best advocate." I imagined Uncle Sam pointing right at me. I really had no idea how to take up this role suddenly bestowed upon me. So began my own journey to find out what advocacy was all about.

Talking Possibilities

Growing up, I knew IEPs meant one thing: frustration. Not only did my brother need specially designed instruction, but my mother was a high school Special Education teacher and talked openly at home about the challenges of writing IEPs and complaining about how my brother's teachers just didn't understand. (Sound familiar?) From this early exposure, I knew I was not cut out to deal with IEPs, or so I thought.

I can't say our first experience in an IEP meeting was comfortable or successful. There we sat; my husband and I doe-eyed and fighting the urge to run. I hated the very thought of being there. Who were all these people, and why was I even sitting in an IEP meeting?

After all, I thought I had made my wishes specifically clear about how our children's lives would play out before they were even born. Let them be who they want to be, but whatever happens, please oh please let them never ever need an IEP. Isn't it funny how life happens?

The very thing we are most afraid of turns up in our lives as if to say, "Here you go, you asked for it."

I disliked that first meeting's experience so much. I knew that if IEPs were going to be our lot in life that I needed to create a new perspective on the whole process. I needed to learn how to get to "yes" at these meetings.

First, I began to read through the pages and pages of evaluations and data collected by strangers about my kids in order to form choices for their Free and Appropriate Public Education or FAPE for you rookies. These pages soon became chapters and volumes housed in two separate three-inch binders. One day, as I was thumbing my way through the pages, it occurred to me these documents represent everything that was wrong with my child. How did we get to feeling and being so WRONG in such a short time? It broke my heart. I placed some pictures in the front of the binder to remind me who my son really was. After all, I may not have known about the importance of bell curves, but I could talk in depth about my son and how he loved flying kites and riding his bike. It was only by accident that these pictures caught the attention of other team members –realizing that they too appreciated knowing who our son was beyond their narrowed and limited versions based on assessments. This interaction was by far the most important in defining our relationship as a team. No longer were we talking percentiles. We talked possibilities and asked questions of one another to match services to the child on the front cover of that thick binder.

Tricks of the Trade: Always be Prepared

Advocacy did not come naturally to me, but the alternative of not raising my voice for others (including my own children!) was simply not an option.

A few years back, Tony Attwood, one of the world's renowned authorities in Asperger's syndrome, came to our tiny burg in Bellingham, WA. As a coordinator for our county's Parent to Parent program I couldn't pass up the chance to see him and learn what I could to help other families. The one thing that stood out for me from his presentation was how important it is to have "tools" when you are in any circumstance. Eventually, this concept got me thinking about my own challenging circumstances with IEPs and my need for helpful tools that would assist me in getting started.

Talking to team members requires both preparation and tact. I found this form I keep close at hand for any occasion: the little black dress of IEPs as I call it. "Preparing for Your Child's IEP" is a basic list I create prior to each child's meeting that helps me sum up where we need to focus. I type it out, make copies and present it to our team and they always welcome this information.

Preparing for Your Child's IEP

- My child is best at:
- My child needs the most help with:
- My child enjoys:
- My child least enjoys:
- My child compares to other children his/her age in these ways:
- My child differs from other children his/her age in these ways:

- When I play or work with my child we usually:
- Help my child has received in the past include:
- Ways I have worked to help my child with behavior or schoolwork that worked are:
- Ways I have worked with my child with behavior or schoolwork that did not work are:
- Special concerns I have about my child are:
- Questions I have about my child's education are:
- Suggestions I have about working with my child are:

Taking it on the Road

Shortly after our children were first diagnosed, I went through advocacy training. When the time came to check the box to become an advocate for a local agency, I declined. I still didn't feel ready. However, just recently a parent called asking for my help. Her daughter was transitioning and she desperately needed someone's supportive hand to guide her. With just a week to prepare, we met and I handed her resource after resource from the Hands & Voices website. I knew it was bordering on overwhelming for her, but there wasn't any time for a slower pace. I instructed her to inform the school team she would be bringing a friend telling her I would be there taking notes. At the meeting the school was VERY curious to know who I was, since Hands & Voices was just becoming known in Washington State.

During the meeting, it was clear how determined this mother was to get her child's unique needs met, but as all of us do especially on a first meeting, she often fought to find the right words that would make an impact on the team. I volleyed a few questions to get the team focused and responding to this student's particular situation. When the reception cooled and the pat answers began, I backed off. I knew this meeting wasn't going to conclude well, and the parent would need to reply by letter afterwards to this team by the way it was proceeding. I kept taking notes. Standing in the parking lot afterwards, with this exhausted mom who was near tears and holding onto her daughter, I recognized that feeling of helplessness and failure I had felt myself at these meetings. This meeting had only been a first step and it killed me to see her doubting herself and asking me "Why didn't you say more?" I gave her a hug and told her we would meet next week to begin her reply. Meanwhile, with her permission, I contacted the professionals servicing her child outside of school asking for back-up. All declined my plea to attend a meeting for various reasons. It was then that I realized just how valuable a parent-led organization like Hands & Voices could be in the day to day lives of families and their children in our state, whose sole allegiance is to the parent and their child.

When the parent and I met again, I had tapped into every resource I knew, both locally and through the Hands & Voices network. We went over the notes from the previous meeting, pulling out useful quotes she could use in her response. It was then that she declared to me she wanted to go for an out of district placement over an hour's drive from their home. My only response was to ground myself in the resources I had gathered doing what was asked of me and pushing through my own self-doubt knowing anything is possible. We crafted a detailed letter stating the child's case and sent it off.

Upon receiving the parent's letter, the school district responded by requesting another meeting. I came prepared with reading glasses, pen and response form in hand ready to take copious notes, when the Special Education director said he was just going to cut to the chase and agree to transfer this child! Stunned, I managed to write on my form just one fabulous word: "YES!"

Advocacy did not come naturally to me, but the alternative of not raising my voice for others (including my own children!) was simply not an option. I've realized through this journey there is so much work to do in our legislation and education in order for systems to recognize the unique needs of each child. After all, none of us dwell in silos, but rather each of our actions, small or large, matters in the bigger picture. To "advocate" just means to speak up on behalf of another. With the support from the H&V network, I have continued to find my own voice and was honored to help another parent find hers.

❝

"It's a dad's job to protect his kids, and this is an area I have always struggled with. We keep them close when they are younger, but as they age, our grasp has to loosen as they figure life out."

Tom Edwards, in a Hands & Voices Communicator article, "Listening to Dads"

The Myth of the Perfect IEP: After the Paperwork is Finished

By Janet DesGeorges, Executive Director, and Karen Putz, Co-Director of Deaf/Hard of Hearing Infusion, Hands & Voices

So... you've gone prepared to your child's IEP meeting and successfully written a plan that creates communication accessibility for your child who is deaf or hard of hearing (d/hh). It's time to bring out the bottle of champagne, right? Not quite! In effect, your work has just begun.

Developing an effective plan of supports and services for the student who is deaf or hard of hearing can be a challenging experience. But even when an appropriate IEP has been developed, there is often a disconnect between the plan and the actual implementation. Many parents, while investing large amounts of time, advocacy, and energy in the actual meeting, fail to follow up to ensure that the IEP is authentically implemented. Some may question whether that is even the parent's role. Isn't it the legal obligation of the school and its personnel to implement the plan that is in place? The answer is a "yes, but...".

One of the areas of IEP plans that parents often don't think about, or fail to participate in, is the actual implementation of their child's IEP. Below are some strategies that you can employ to ensure that follow-up is happening, to understand who is responsible when a support or service is not implemented, and how to 'manage' the players in order to facilitate cohesion among an IEP team. Even when an IEP team is functioning and collaborating with one another throughout the school day, parents are often not called in until there is a problem. You can help to build a team where you are an equal and effective partner.

Parents As Team Managers: Who's on your team? MVP'S

Think about every member of your child's IEP team. The IDEA requires that the members of the IEP team include: The parents, at least one regular ed. Teacher, at least one special ed. Teacher, a representative of the local educational agency, an individual who can interpret the instructional implications of evaluation results, and at the discretion of the parent or agency, other individuals who have knowledge or special expertise regarding the child, including related services personnel as appropriate; and the child with a disability, whenever appropriate. (20 U.S.C. 1414(d)(B) (i-vii)).

Among the team that is assembled to deliver the services and supports for your child throughout the year, there is often an MVP-- that professional who goes the extra mile, who supports you when you are advocating for your child, who you tend to call on when there is a problem. Whether that person is your child's general ed. teacher, sign language interpreter, teacher of the deaf/hh or a speech language pathologist, you can create and sustain a positive relationship throughout the year by communicating regularly, contacting them when there are things to be celebrated, and not just complaints to be delivered etc. and to be able to create strategies for effective communication access.

If you can't think of one person on your child's IEP that you would consider an MVP, start thinking about who you could begin a positive relationship with in order to be able to collaborate with throughout the year, and be able to call upon for help when something falls through the cracks.

MVP Case Study: 4th Grade student Emily shows up for Physical Education class (PE). The PE teacher refuses to wear the FM system, as she is afraid it will get broken. She states, "Anyway, "PE is such a visual thing, Emily will 'catch on' to what's going on." Emily comes home and tells Mom. Mom calls the school and gets the runaround. She then calls the Itinerant teacher of the Deaf, someone Mom can always count on, who shows up at the school the next day, and sets up a meeting with the PE teacher. She provides information so that the PE teacher understands that the lack of communication accessibility without the use of the FM is unacceptable, and in violation of Emily's IEP. The PE teacher wears the FM system later that day, and for the rest of the year..

Working collaboratively

You cannot expect the team to have a two-hour meeting, (the annual IEP review) and be ready to go out and 'play' the whole season without maintaining collaboration. As the team manager, it may be up to you to set up an email listserv, phone tree, face-to-face individual or team meetings throughout the year to maintain collaboration and the big-picture implementation of services. One of the outcomes of the annual meeting should be an understanding of how the team will communicate throughout the year with one another, as well as keeping the parent in the loop. It is often a good idea during the IEP meeting to document how this communication will take place and how often it is expected.

Collaboration Case Study: Mrs. Martin initiates and meets with each member of the IEP team throughout the year at the school or the local coffee shop. They discuss current concerns, celebrations, and new ideas to assure appropriate education services are being delivered. One of the concerns that Mrs. Martin's 6th grade son has expressed is 'none of my teachers ever remember to repeat the questions the other students are asking'. When Mrs. Martin meets with the interpreter, they discuss ways in which the interpreter can continue to monitor and remind the teachers to repeat the questions, and also to be aware to make sure that every question is interpreted fully. Mrs. Martin talks to her son about his right to ask for information to be repeated. Her son is also assigned a deaf/hh role model through the state role model program who helps him to gain confidence in self-advocacy, and to understand his rights to communication access.

Ensuring quality control

One of the most effective ways to feel assured as a parent of 'quality control' of the implementation of the IEP is to volunteer at school. Parents have often stated that what looked really good on paper in the IEP meeting didn't seem to be playing out in 'day to day operations' when they were actually in the classroom. Most of the time it is not intentional, but with another pair of eyes occasionally in the classroom, a parent is able to ensure that what the teacher of the deaf knows is what the general ed teacher knows is what the speech therapist knows is what the interpreter knows, etc. Another result of volunteering at the school is that relationships in your school community can grow as a product of your direct involvement. For instance, the principal of a school is more likely to respond to a parent's concern who has 'shown her face' in the school and has contributed to its well-being through volunteering.

While volunteering in the classroom is a good thing to do, a parent can't be in the classroom all the time, and as the child grows older, it becomes less feasible to be in the classroom. We must teach our children self - advocacy skills so that they are comfortable with ensuring appropriate access. The IEP team should not expect the student to have to constantly be monitoring IEP compliance, but the student should feel comfortable raising their hand to remind the teacher to turn on the FM, or to make sure they've delivered a hard copy of the notes, or to remind the interpreter they can't see them in front of a window, etc. The development of self-advocacy skills is a critical component of growth for deaf and hard of hearing children. Your child is an important link in discovering if changes need to be made. Connect with your child on a regular basis. Through conversations with your child, you may discover that the school allowed an intern to replace the regular interpreter for a week. You may discover social situations happening on the playground that need to be addressed. That being said, there shouldn't be an undue burden on the child to ensure compliance - that's what the team is there for.

Case Study: A school ordered a new, wireless FM system for a young student at the start of the school year. Midway through the school year, the itinerant teacher discovered that the student's FM system was not working. The parents consulted an educational audiologist who noticed that the student's hearing aid did not have an internal wiring component that was compatible with the FM system. As a result, the student had gone without a working FM system since the beginning of the school year.

Parents need to ensure that the actual implementation of services is written on the IEP. Services should be written in a way that shows who will be responsible for checking equipment (educational audiologist, itinerant teacher?) and how frequently it will be checked.

Even when you are assured that the team has done their job, you may find situations that are overlooked. For example, the use of captioned videos and films may be indicated on the IEP. Itinerant teachers may give in-services in the beginning of the year, familiarizing teachers with closed captioning and the resources for captioned films. Later in the year, you may discover that the music teacher was showing a series of films on famous musicians, without the benefit of captioning, unaware of access to captioned resources that could be substituted. In some instances, you may have new teachers coming in during the middle of the school year or long-term substitute teachers. Parents can collaborate with the team when new situations arise and request in-services for the change of staff.

Your Rights under the Law

Sometimes, even when you've done all the right things, compliance is still a problem. What are your rights under the law? While the law does not require that any agency, teacher, or other person be held accountable if a child does not achieve the growth projected in the annual goals and benchmarks, they must still make a good faith effort to assist the child to achieve the goals and objectives or benchmarks listed in the IEP. (sec. 300.350(a)(b)). Sometimes though, there are blatant omissions (i.e. an interpreter is listed as a service provider, and no interpreter is hired). A parent can file a signed written complaint under the procedures outlined in the IDEA. You can request these procedures from your school district, and find out more information about your rights under the law at www.wrightslaw.org

When It's Working Right

A thirteen year old hard of hearing student comes home every day with all the homework assignments for the day clearly understood. Her general ed teacher announces the homework assignment to the class while facing the student, with the FM system turned on. (This teacher went through two in-service meetings with the itinerant teacher of the deaf, and also watched a video on communication access). She then turns around and writes the assignment on the board, giving the student visual access. If the student missed anything, she can turn to the interpreter for clarification. Later in the day, the special ed resource teacher in the building sends an email to the parent (this happens every day) to let her know what homework assignments are due the next day. The parent plays his part by asking the student what needs to be done, checking the email from the resource teacher, and helping the student with homework when necessary. (This is a true story.)

When everyone on the IEP team does their part, it's like watching a team make the perfect play. To get it right often takes a lot of time and practice, but the outcome is worth it. Our kids deserve appropriate education help when they need it, and everyone doing their best.

Over the years, the members of the IEP team change, but parents remain the steady, constant factor in their child's lifelong case management. When it comes to your child, no one else can keep his eye on the big picture quite like you, the parent. It is your ability to see the high school graduate in the bassinette that will ultimately ensure that the journey is a successful one.

"

Education is a shared commitment between dedicated teachers, motivated students, and enthusiastic parents with high expectations.

Bob Beauprez

Ephphatha

By Dr. Thomas Caulfield

When the pediatric audiologist informed us that our twelve-month-old son was profoundly Deaf, I found myself standing there confused and overwhelmed.

I knew one thing for certain: our life was about to get very hard.

Almost like a movie, the scenes began to play out, and at that early moment in time, just after Christopher's diagnosis, I began to write. I knew what we were about to experience would be challenging and I wanted to capture it all. The journals I kept were the genesis of a book I have written (published with the same title). Writing came easily at first, but later, in the most difficult times, it also was unbearable. Thankfully, there were intermittent periods when things were going our way and we actually started having experiences that somewhat resembled those of other families. But challenges seemed always lurking, ready to strike: we had serious medical complications that required us to travel coast to coast for treatment.

Besides the medical challenges, we faced a similar wrestling match with the educational system. Whose right was it to choose the intervention strategies that would best help Christopher? As Christopher aged, I could see another battle looming on the horizon. The support services center in our city had given our family commendable help up until Christopher turned three. After that birthday, however, things changed.

With his implant, Christopher could now hear sounds at twenty-five to thirty decibels. (Without the implant, his decibel level skyrocketed to one hundred and ten, hearing sounds as loud as a jet engine.) Since most people hear at about twenty decibels, we felt confident he could handle the challenge of communicating orally. But the city's support services did not believe in this teaching method. They stood on their methodology working exclusively with sign language, and we wanted to try oral education. It soon became clear that my wife and I were philosophically opposed to this latest support service group's only teaching methodology.

Candidly, I knew we were up against incredible odds when a Catholic nun with more than fifty years of Deaf education to her credit told me, "Dr. Caulfield, in all my years, I am not sure I have seen a family so relentlessly try to combat all the hardships that come with raising a child with such a profound disability." She counseled me to pace myself, adding that if I did choose to scale back my efforts, I could one day look back and honestly say that a great deal had been accomplished. The day she spoke to me, I felt like I was out on a limb cutting with a saw and found myself on the wrong side of the tree branch.

We turned for support to the Alexander Graham Bell Association, an internationally known nonprofit group that emphasizes helping Deaf children to thrive in mainstream society. We also sought the help of attorneys committed to fighting for children with disabilities. When the dust settled, we were extremely happy: we would be able to teach our son in the way we felt was best.

Through it all I continued to write. In one particularly tough period, I remember wanting to post a big, bold warning: If you keep reading this journal, be advised it is not for the faint of heart.

Maybe simply by the grace of God, Christopher turned out to be a phenomenal athlete. With those basketball talents came all sorts of rights and privileges that he as a Deaf kid never knew existed. Combined with that athletic prowess was Christopher's incredible horsepower academically. With our student athlete by our side, resilience fueled us to combat all of our social, medical, legal, and religious hardships.

As we battled, I continued to write, and as we endured for another decade, I knew the important thing to capture was not who was right within our circumstances but rather what was true. So, we persevered, all the while keeping faith that eventually our path would "be opened"—ephphatha—and we could make our way. And maybe when it was all over, our wish would be to have enough resilience remaining in our spirit to bring hope and assistance to others struggling in their own lives.

Christopher is who he is today because of our relentless efforts to never give up as his advocates. He entered the B. Thomas College of Computing and Informational Sciences at Rochester Institute of Technology in New York. While at RIT he studied web and mobile computing with a concentration in human computer interaction and ubiquitous computing, along with an immersion in Deaf Cultural studies.

Throughout his college career, Christopher continued to be extensively involved in his community. He was active in both the Newman and Cru campus ministries and was also a member of Sigma Chi fraternity. He served RIT's residential life program as a resident advisor for three straight years on campus. During his junior and senior years, he was a research assistant and later a teaching assistant for the College of Computing. He also secured highly sought-after summer internships in New York, Washington, D.C., and Lincoln, Nebraska. His summer project work encompassed user-centered research and design in areas of commercial business, government, and sports world technologies.

Christopher is extremely proud of his research work in the Linguistic and Assistive Technologies Laboratory at RIT. He believes that innovation in linguistic technologies and computer interaction could empower and create more possibilities for people. He hopes that, through his efforts, the lives of people with disabilities will also be made easier through accessibility applications. Christopher graduated cum laude from RIT and went on to Cornell for his graduate studies that fall.

Always remember: Everyone has the right to be understood!!

A story about Christopher playing basketball:
https://www.espn.com/mens-college-basketball/columns/story?-columnist=oneil_dana&id=6125964

Chris, at RIT, looks back at high school:
https://www.youtube.com/watch?v=exs3-zE6Zjs&sns=em:

*Under Title II of the ADA, **schools
must**, without charge, ensure that
communication with students
with disabilities is **as effective**
as communication with students
without disabilities, **giving primary
consideration to students and parents**
in determining which auxiliary aids
and services are necessary to provide such
effective communication.*

From the U.S. Department of Justice
& the U.S. Department of Education
Policy Guidance, November 12, 2014

The Key Steps to Advocating for Your Child

Reprinted with permission from Deaf Child Australia

As a parent group in Australia, we have learned these tips over the years that other parents may find helpful. Many parents of deaf children find themselves in situations where they need to advocate on behalf of their child. Advocacy means to 'stand beside' someone. Families may need to negotiate for resources or support for their deaf child when they believe that things 'are not quite right,' or when people who hold the resources don't see that things are not quite right.

Perhaps you find yourself in a situation where you feel things are 'not quite right.' What can you do? You could:

- Walk away from the situation
- Fight it head on
- Deny the situation, or
- Decide to get some modification or improvement to the situation. It is when we feel that we need to get some improvement happening that advocacy begins.

What are the stages of advocacy?

Advocacy may occur at different levels.

- Advocacy to set the scene: e.g., some parents work at creating an environment where others will have more understanding of the needs of their deaf child. This involves explaining your child's needs and making sure that people working with your child understand what the potential barriers are and how to support your child over them.

- Advocacy through meetings: e.g., parents have the opportunity to participate and plan their child's individual education plan. This often requires discussion of specific learning needs and concerns and having your position heard. You may also organize meetings to discuss progress and monitor how well your deaf child's needs are being addressed.

- Raising the profile of advocacy: sometimes you may need to take the issues further, that is, to take stronger steps and to get the support of people who are able to release resources or expertise to meet your child's needs. In a school setting this may involve meetings with the school principal or writing letters to the regional director of education (or equivalent), outlining your child's needs and advocating for a serious look at how to improve the opportunities for your child.

- For a few, there will be situations where all the advocacy effort has not delivered the needed responses, and then you will need to consider whether it is time to take the issue to a systemic level for action.

Key Steps in Advocacy

When advocating for your deaf child, you will need to consider these steps below, so that a positive outcome for everyone can be achieved.

1. Define the situation - Ask yourself, or others:

- What is it that your child or family needs? What are the issues? How can you prioritize these issues?

- How is the situation best approached? Is it through meetings, through informal discussions?

- Who is involved in the situation?

- Where is the issue occurring?

- What are my goals in this process?

- What is the common ground of everyone involved? How can this common ground be found and used to achieve the best results for my child?

2. Information

You need to find out as much information as you can. Information could include things such as:

- Your rights, e.g., the Disability Discrimination Act, Educational Department Guidelines, UN Declaration of Human Rights
- Learning as much as you can about the problem or situation and arguments people may use against you
- knowing who is responsible for change
- knowing the available support services
- knowing the organizations that support families for children with disabilities, e.g., Deaf Children Australia, Association of Children with a Disability, Hands & Voices, etc.
- Sharing information with the people involved
- Documenting everything that is said or written and keeping all these documents.

3. Communication and interpersonal skills

It is very important that you keep communication open and friendly so that you do not create an additional barrier. You can do this by:

- respecting each other
- listening to others
- being open to others
- using empathy
- using negotiation
- being clear in what you say and want
- collaborating with others
- using encouragement when people try to meet your needs

4. Energy

You will need energy. For some people, the role of advocate comes easily. For others it's more difficult. The trick is to know when you have the energy and when you don't, and to identify the best person to help you. If you need another person to assist you, choose this person wisely and make sure they have the knowledge and skills to assist you.

This article was reprinted with permission from Deaf Children Australia, at: https://www.deafchildrenaustralia.org.au/

For over 12 years, I have felt completely and utterly alone while navigating how to best serve my son. That all changed when my audiologist gave me a referral to Hands & Voices. When I looked over the information the Parent Guide had sent on typical accommodations, I began to cry. My son is not alone. I am not alone. The things I ask for from his school are not absurd or far-reaching. They are quite normal. The "quirks" that my son has are related to his (unilateral) hearing loss. I honestly saw a light at the end of a very dark tunnel.

Libby Robinson, parent of a child with a unilateral hearing loss in a military family

Advocating for Eligibility When There are "*No Concerns*"

By Janet DesGeorges

"**D**uring the eligibility process for IEP services, everyone is saying my daughter is not eligible for services. I agree with them that so far, the assessments being used are not showing educational impact.... I also feel the team is trying to assess her appropriately, and yet, my gut keeps telling me that something is just not right, and I can't figure out how to address this...what should I do?"

I have many titles I can think of in the work I do at Hands & Voices. One of the titles I am most proud of (besides being a mom of a deaf daughter, of course!) is the role I have played over the years in being an educational advocate. For over 15 years, I have attended over 60 I.E.P. meetings with families as a lay advocate. The issue of eligibility for IDEA services has been at the forefront in recent years. With the advent of universal newborn hearing screening, children identified earlier may not be showing the same types of deficits as in previous generations. Eligibility has some very strong 'objective' measures that must be met, along with some subjective elements that are sometimes not always easily measured or accounted for.

This story comes from an advocacy situation in which a family contacted me after two eligibility meetings they had completed with their school district – and were at an impasse.

To be honest, most phone calls from families asking for an advocate usually start at a very high level of emotion. Typically, families call on the support of advocates when there is disagreement, often in a contentious atmosphere. I've learned over the years to begin conversations with families by letting them share everything going on, and then begin to process what parts of the situation are relational, (between IEP team members and the family), whether there are other things going on beyond the needs of the individual student, (i.e. money, power, philosophical or methodological disagreements) and then work with the family on how to get to 'yes' in conversations with I.E.P. teams in areas that are important for student success.

But from the outset, this advocacy situation was different. The parents, when they called, felt that the school district truly was working towards the best interests of their daughter. However, the parents had a 'gut instinct' that all was not on target for their young child with a mild hearing level.

The following, based on a true case (name of family has been changed) highlights the story of a student 'doing really well' and at the same time parent's wanting to address significant needs that to date had not been uncovered in typical assessment procedures. This case uniquely considers some state-level eligibility criteria from the state in which it occurred at the time, but would be similar to the two-prong eligibility under IDEA: 1) have a qualifying condition, i.e., a disability as defined by law in statute CDR 300.8(c) and 2) must need specialized instruction in order to get the benefit of his/her education.

The Morrell Story

The Morell family felt their hard-of-hearing daughter, Kirstin, would need special education services as she entered kindergarten. She had previously been determined ineligible during her pre-school years and had been attending a private pre-school. Because Kirstin had been doing well in most areas of development and scored within normal ranges in assessment tests (doing well academically; no major speech/language concerns/ good self-advocacy) the school district's position was that there were no grounds for qualification.

According to the state's legal requirements for IEP eligibility, Kirstin had a qualifying hearing loss, but the district IEP team could not find any delays or prove a loss of educational benefit that would justify the need for specialized instruction.

The Morell's felt very strongly that they were seeing some delays in Kirstin's language, speech articulation, self-advocacy/self-awareness, and social/emotional areas in their child.

However, the IEP team members from the district would not corroborate these concerns either through teacher observation and/or standardized testing. The parents also desired that their daughter be in a program where there were peers who were also deaf/hard of hearing.

When the educational audiologist reported on Kirstin's *Functional Listening Evaluation (FLE), (Johnson, 2013), she reported that there were definite 'inconsistencies' with Kirstin's listening perception in the different conditions assessed. (e.g., noise, distance from the talker, no visual cues, different settings) When the team reconsidered the "inattentive, inconsistent, and/or inappropriate classroom behavior, (the direct language used from the educational impact section in that state's law) the word inconsistent stood out to the team. Although the student was doing well, her ability to access communication across all settings throughout the day had to be addressed.

The nuances of access for a D/HH child are often overlooked when a student who does well in a quiet situation is often assumed to have the same success in noise, at a distance from the talker, and/or in poor acoustical situations. (e.g., cafeteria, gyms). The team began to acknowledge through the objective data of the FLE that this was not true for Kirstin, even with her mild hearing loss. Interestingly, the very team that had been downplaying gaps in their test scores found themselves actively engaged in identifying necessary supports and services for Kirstin once eligibility via the FLE was established. They began to address the other needs that her parents had been advocating for including social and emotional support. The door of eligibility was open, and an appropriate IEP was developed to address Kirsten's needs, including a school placement decision enabling her to benefit from additional staff resources and D/HH peers in critical mass at the district's center-based program.

As the years went by, the student remained at the center-based program and thrived academically, socially, and emotionally. Today she is a bright, successful student with a great future ahead of her.

The FLE is a powerful tool to show that there is no such thing as a static hearing loss. Audiograms do not tell the whole story. Even though a child is "doing well," communication accessibility is imperative for D/HH children, and that often requires specialized instruction, adaptations, and flexibility across different environments. A 504 plan might be the answer for some D/HH students, but the nuances of meeting that child's needs throughout the day, including social and academic implications of accessibility are usually best articulated and implemented via an IEP.

This story highlights for me as an advocate that 'no' does not always mean 'no'; that parents know their child best and to persevere even when a child is passing grade to grade without apparent deficits – to be diligent in ensuring accessibility and supports when needed. I am reminded of this section of the Federal Office of Special Education Programs (OSEP) policy response in policy clarification letter that can be used in situations like this:

"...It remains the Department's position that the term "educational performance" as used in the IDEA and its implementing regulations is not limited to academic performance. Whether a speech and language impairment adversely affects a child's educational performance must be determined on a case-by-case basis, depending on the unique needs of a particular child, and not based only on discrepancies in age or grade performance in academic subject areas. Section 614(b)(2)(A) of IDEA and the final regulations at 34 CFR § 300.304(b) state that in conducting an evaluation, the public agency must use a variety of assessment tools and strategies to gather relevant functional, developmental, and academic information. Therefore, IDEA and the regulations clearly establish that the determination about whether a child is a child with a disability is not limited to information about the child's academic performance. Furthermore, 34 CFR § 300.101(c) states that each State must ensure that a free appropriate public education (FAPE) is available to any individual child with a disability who needs special education and related services, even though the child has not failed or been retained in a course or grade, and is advancing from grade to grade." – (OSEP Letter to Clarke 2007)

*The functional listening evaluation is available at https://www. handsandvoices.org/pdf/func_eval.pdf

* PLAAFP (quote on next page) stands for **Present Level of Academic Achievement and Functional Performance**. Some states/districts refer to it as PLAAFP, some as PLOP and some as PLP. This section servces as a starting point for the coming year's IEP, or Individualized Educational Program.

*If it feels like the assessment results reported on the IEP looked at your child through a straw, you are probably right. A good *PLAAFP requires asking the **right** questions and using multiple sources of data to answer them.*

Susan Elliott, Ph.D.

Coulda, Shoulda, Wouldas: A Transition Story

By Amy Scriven

"**H**ow weird do you want me to be, mom?" My son is the sweetest, most polite teenager, who would never say that to my face, but I could tell from his sadness and frustration that he was thinking it. "Hearing aids? I don't need them; I've been fine this far in life. IEP? No way, mom!" Unspoken, heartbreaking words written all over his face and through his future actions of refusing to wear his aids, hiding his mini mic, and feelings of shame and sadness from being what he would call different.

Late Identified.

We intended to adopt a baby, but fell in love with Luke, age 14. and rearranged our lives for a teenager, who spoke no English and had significant medical needs. Once home with Luke, even though we had never met Cole, we learned that Luke had been friends with Cole in the orphanage. We tried to help find Cole a forever family. We had known about Cole even before we realized he and Luke were friends, through an amazing young man from Ireland who attempted for many years to help Cole find a family. Age 14 is the last stop for orphans from China; at 14 China no longer allows them to be adopted. Staff at the orphanage told us that Cole wanted so much to be adopted and was sad to see his friends leave him behind one-by-one as they found homes. Nine months later, with two weeks to go, we found ourselves on a plane rushing to adopt our precious Cole before he turned 14. Once again, God gave us another brand-new 14-year-old son who spoke no English and had significant medical needs.

It took a few years to uncover all of Cole's medical needs, including that he is hard of hearing and the subsequent recommendation of hearing aids. As parents we think, "Okay, this is costly, but not bad, there is a solution, we can navigate this." Our teen was thinking, "Whoa no way, hold it right there, cowboy. Hearing aids in high

school? No way!" Our son went through all the stages of grief over his need for hearing aids, and as uneducated parents, we struggled to guide and comfort him.

High School IEPs.

I'm at the age where doctors suggest mammograms and colonoscopies, both are more desirable than navigating an IEP meeting. Our first denial of an IEP cited that our son did not qualify because his IQ scores were too high, and English is his second language, which was deemed the sole contributor to his struggles. The fact he was hard of hearing was skimmed over and labeled, "not that significant," without even showing us the legal criteria for eligibility. I was crushed and cried at the end of the meeting when Cole was denied IEP accommodations. Yes, our son is smart, yes English is his second language, but the poor dude couldn't understand the teachers well enough to acquire English at the rate that matched his IQ. My biggest mistake, among many, was not seeking out an advocate specifically for deaf/hard of hearing kids.

My list of Coulda, Shoulda, Wouldas:

1. **Seek help from advocates who specialize in kids who are deaf/ hard of hearing.** Not only did the Hands & Voices team assist me with understanding the IEP process, my son's rights, how an IEP could help him, but they also guided me emotionally and educationally through hearing loss in general. As a mom of a late identified kiddo, I didn't fully understand how to read an audiogram, let alone effectively navigate IDEA laws. The Colorado Hands & Voices team spent hours at my kitchen table, over the phone, and through email helping me learn and prepare. Their coaching helped me to be more confident during the IEP meeting and provided my mama heart with some much-needed love, reassurance, and tender care during what was a confusing time for our family.

2. **Be open to advice.** Our son Cole, who is now 18 and much farther along in this journey, does not mind me sharing that he did everything that first year to foil efforts to assist with his ability to communicate and gather information. My response to his actions, which was all part of his grieving process, often made the situations worse. The Hands & Voices team gave both my husband and me, and the IEP team, suggestions to help Cole feel more comfortable speaking up for the accommodations he needs to learn at the rate of his peers. For example, allowing Cole more control over his hearing aid usage, setting up a plan for a period of months where his teachers discreetly prompted Cole for his mini-mic instead of putting the responsibility solely on Cole, and having him meet with a teacher of the deaf/hard of hearing to research and learn about his hearing levels and how to advocate for his needs.

3. **Come to the IEP meeting with a plan**. Research IDEA laws as it pertains to students who are deaf/hard of hearing, create a list of your teenager's areas of need with specific examples from both home and school. Also, come prepared with a list of possible accommodations you would like to see for your teen once the IEP is approved. Practice how to describe your concerns to the team and your answers to possible objections. Remember, as a parent

your opinion matters, and what you see at home is as valid as the perception in the classroom.

4. **Identify the specific criteria for qualification.** One of my most significant mistakes was to not obtain a blank copy of the IEP determination forms before the meeting. During the meeting, possibly because of a lack of understanding about deaf and hard of hearing needs, the team never showed my husband the criteria for qualifying. Since I had not looked at the specific requirements, and only the broad categories, I took the team at their word when they asked/said, "We don't think he will qualify based on this, right?" Cole has additional needs, so I simply figured he would qualify under a different category, which in my ignorance at the time was just fine with me. Unfortunately, the team convinced me he didn't qualify under any categories, and I was too shocked and exhausted to realize we needed to back up and review the details of each category. Prior review of the details might have provided me with enough information to say, "Hold it right there, partner, Cole qualifies because of X and X."

5. **Do not underestimate the impact being hard of hearing can have the ability to acquire education.** IEPs are not just for kids who are intellectually disabled. Often educators are so used to assisting kiddos who need special education services, because of cognitive delays or disabilities, that they fail to see or understand that kids who are smart, or even gifted and talented, benefit from an IEP when they have other needs, such as those who are deaf or hard of hearing. In my son's case, the educators were convinced his hearing aids were 'good enough', and helped him hear and understand the teacher. Not only were they overestimating what aids can and cannot provide, but they were also overlooking my son's other medical needs that complicate his ability to hear, and his decision to not wear his aids and hide them or his mini-mic. Additionally, Cole refused to explain to anyone that he was hard of hearing. The team did not realize how a Teacher of the Deaf could teach him about his level of hearing and how to explain it to educators, peers, and even future bosses his unique needs. A Teacher of the Deaf could also help Cole pick a seat placement

in the classroom most appropriate for him, as well as assisting him with some speech and language issues. Instead, any difficulty was attributed to English as a second language, but actually was linked to missing words and inflection as a result of being hard of hearing. My lack of understanding of all of this as a new mom of a kiddo who is hard of hearing was detrimental to acquiring an IEP and getting Cole services to help him acquire education at the same rate of his peers. I needed someone to explain all of this to me so that I could educate the IEP team. Praise God for the Hands & Voices advocates who helped me outline the services that Cole would benefit from and in addition ways we could better assist him in our home.

6. **Consider speaking with the IEP team without your teenager.** Cole is a joy to parent. He's easy-going, quick to laugh, and if we are being totally transparent a real mama's boy. However, he did not think he needed aids for hearing or an IEP. During the first meeting, not only did the educator's cite Cole's insistence of not needing help but also, Cole had to hear over and over my words of how he was not thriving and not performing as well as he could in school. This sent the wrong message to Cole that he was somehow failing, which he was not, and that he was responsible for this perceived failure. One solution is to conduct part of the meeting without your teen. Take a bit of time to review your concerns with the team, and then have your teen join after for the solutions and accommodations portion, so that he or she can feel empowered rather than deflated.

7. **Plan for transition services.** Your IEP team should document transition plans starting at 16, but I found my son still needed assistance answering the big question, "What's next after high school?" Expand outside of the IEP team meetings, and attend workshops designed to help you and your child determine areas of interest and the proper track for exploration. The path ahead may include college, Vocational Rehabilitation assistance with training and job coaching, or perhaps volunteering for more discovery. You are not alone, there are many organizations that provide transitional information, including Hands & Voices.

A year later, armed with copious amounts of research and knowledgeable advocates from Hands & Voices, Cole was approved for an IEP that is helping him to understand his teachers and material better, learn to self-advocate, and educate his peers. Most importantly, Cole's starting to see himself not as weird, or different, but just as our precious Cole, who truly is a gift from God.

Sample plan we presented at the IEP determination meeting:

	Accommodation	Comments
Physical Arrangements & Technology	Provide remote mic or DM/FM as needed.	Contingent upon student's utilization of hearing aids/ equipment. Needs adult support for this.
	Flexible seating - Closer/to near the teacher/speaker, away from background noise, etc. Student can move as needed based on need.	Needs adult support. Consult with PT/OT regarding swivel support since Cole can't easily turn to find a speaker.
	Flashing fire alarms, smoke detectors, and noise reduction in the classroom working in hallway with partner, etc.	Student needs adult support in noisy environments to help him remain engaged.
	Access to audio books through the school Bookshare account.	Adding auditory support coupled with written documentation significantly bolsters student comprehension.

	Accommodation	Comments
Lesson Presentation	Open ended questions for comprehension and recall.	Examples: What did you hear? What's next? Frequent walk-bys to ensure understanding of expectations, time limits, and content.
	Making sure directions are understood	Provide visual and auditory support due to a combination of language and hearing.
	Class notes, slides, and supporting document provided	Student can't take notes during instruction. Notes benefit the student and parents to support homework.
	Visual supplements to increase comprehension.	Universal design for learning (UDL) assists all students.
	Teachers should repeat/ rephrase what students say in the classroom.	Adds incidental learning from peers
	Allow extra time for processing information.	
	Gain student's attention prior to speaking.	
Test Taking	Encourage use of wireless device for amplification for computer tests	
	Check for understanding of any oral instructions for tests or quizzes.	

	Accommodation	Comments
Critical Areas for Success	The student will understand the impact of hearing difference, understand how to navigate education, safety, community skills, social skills, communication repair/speech.	Specialized instruction areas
	Support self-advocacy	Provide opportunities for the student to role play introduction to new teacher with accommodations, when equipment (FM, hearing aids, etc.) malfunctions, when he doesn't understand, etc.

"

Professionals need to be willing to learn from each other as they value the importance of viewing the whole child.

Dinah Beams

The Puzzle of Deafness and Autism

By LaShawna Sims

I have heard that often times the first deaf or hard of hearing person some people meet is their own deaf or hard of hearing child. While for us that wasn't the case, we had a similar experience with a different diagnosis. We have two boys who are both severe to profoundly deaf and bilateral cochlear implant users. Our youngest son Logan also has autism.

We knew one person with autism. All we knew of autism was what we saw in that one individual. I remember telling myself things like; no, our youngest doesn't act the same way or do the same things that person does. I remember thinking that we just didn't get him enough social time with others since his big brother started school. His progress, or lack thereof, in speech was fine. We were told that

not all children with cochlear implants progress at the same speed. The professionals advised us not to compare the two brothers' progress in speech.

What are we seeing?

A common question we asked ourselves in our home was, "Is this autism, the hearing loss or just him being a kid?" Our son was diagnosed as "moderate" and "high-functioning" on the autism spectrum. He is also non-verbal but uses some American Sign Language (ASL) and the Picture Exchange Communication System (PECS) to communicate with us. Over the years, his receptive language skills blossomed. Most days he wears his CIs with no issues. Other days, he knocks them off as if they are causing discomfort. It is often hard to determine whether or not he is having a "sensory moment" because of the autism, being a "typical" child who is having a moment of defiance, or if there is something wrong with his cochlear implant processors (CIs). What is he trying to tell us?

I like to say there is a lot of troubleshooting that goes on with our son. Some days he is happy to put his CIs on, while other days it can be a bit of a tug of war. I have a hard time sometimes "making" him put his CIs on, because I feel like I am not being mindful of his autism diagnosis and what effects the "silence to instant sound" may have on him sometimes. Because his expressive language is still progressing, it can be a challenge to know exactly what is going on with him. He can let us know in sign or with PECS that he is hurt, sad, calm, or silly and wiggly. But when it comes to expressing exactly WHY he is feeling those ways, we aren't always sure.

In the past, Logan has never really gotten a good "MAP" for his CIs and we think that is due to his autism diagnosis. Getting him to reliably respond to any sounds he is hearing has been a work in progress. Before he was identified with autism, I dreaded going to the audiologist because it was a literal "WWE wrestling match" trying to hold him down just to run an impedance test. I can remember making sure that I wore clothes that would allow me to wrestle with him and not look completely disheveled after the appointment. Leaving those appointments, I would feel so defeated. I'd feel like I was a terrible

parent for forcing him to go through the appointment. Then on the flip side, I knew that I wanted him to have as much good access to sound as possible because that is what he needed if we wanted him to eventually use spoken language. For several years, all of his "maps" were manually made and set very conservatively.

Once we got the autism diagnosis, things changed for the better. His behaviors all began to make sense. We started ABA (Applied Behavior Analysis) therapy for him. His therapists have been quite accommodating in respecting our wishes incorporating ASL in his therapy for communication. None of his therapists knew one sign in ASL before starting with us. Now, many of them have been inspired to learn more ASL and even use it with some of their other nonverbal clients. We've even had much better success at the audiologist! I can happily say that I no longer have to wear my "wrestling" attire to an appointment. With the help of his ABA therapists, we have worked on "mock audiology appointments" which have proven to be success-ful for Logan. He has gotten the best "maps" he has ever had in his initial years of having cochlear implants.

As you can see, advocating for Logan's individual needs is so import-ant. We approach advocacy with a teamwork mentality. We take in and apply what the specialist suggests. If we think using what we've learned from the specialist could be enhanced with our ideas, we speak up and suggest it. It is okay to speak up for him while still being respectful of the specialist's expertise. As parents living with a child with a dual diagnosis, you become the expert on your child. Being open, making suggestions and sharing information with our child's specialists, has proven to be effective for our son. At the end of the day, it's all about Logan and we are all on the same team.

While things are progressively getting better, we still have our struggles. We are learning together as a family. It's not easy to pick apart which diagnosis is causing whatever action, feeling or emotion he may be experiencing. All we can do is take it day by day and one step at a time. In all of those hours and steps, we revel in the fact that he is uniquely him and we love every little thing about him. It makes us stronger as individuals and stronger as a family. Even though we have had some hard days, it is gratifying to look back at those struggles and celebrate how far Logan has come. It's a great reminder that despite our current struggle, we will overcome it together as a family. For that, we are blessed and grateful for this unique journey.

Who knows where our children would be today if they didn't have someone fighting for them, seeking services, or imparting help from the very beginning?

Bailey Vincent

Advocating for Parent Choice

By Katie Bishop

O ur story is one of passion, preparation, and teamwork. We started our journey to transition our son into preschool when he was just a year old. Yes, at age one. I know that seems extreme, but we felt it was necessary. My husband and I had just enrolled our son into a special educational program for children like ours with multicomplex needs. He already had an Individualized Family Service Plan (IFSP) in place. We knew that an Individual Education Plan (IEP) was to come, we knew that Child Find would be part of the process, and as an employee working in special education for fifteen years, I knew this was not going to be an easy transition. We started to prepare early.

Born with multiple needs, our son was in and out of the hospital for the first two years of his life. He was late-identified with hearing loss: progressive mild/moderate in his right ear and moderate/severe in his left ear. His other needs include mobility (fine and gross motor), respiratory, feeding and vision needs. All these factors were at the forefront of our minds as our son's transition into preschool neared. We made calls, talked to other parents, followed blogs, read articles, read books and asked our learning specialist at our current school questions almost daily regarding the transition process in anticipation of what lay ahead. Three years later, as I sat at our son's graduation from his program that July, I realized that those "next steps" in the journey had arrived. The beginning of his educational career was just months away. Though we anticipated a fight, little did we know just how tough the fight would be.

We were advised to call Child Find that December to get on their calendar. Child Find told us that it was too early and to call back in the new year. We called in January; they told us to call back in March. Frustrated and feeling pushed aside, we were not willing to

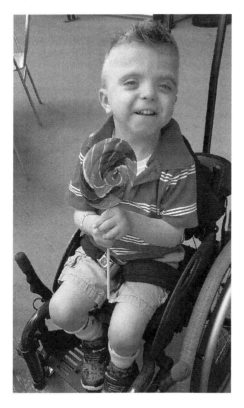

wait. We called again in February. Other parents were enrolling their students into their school of choice. Why couldn't we? We started to question how parent choice would work for us as parents with a child of multicomplex needs. Would we have a choice? We finally got on the Child Find calendar for April. Then the district called and said some of the essential team members from Child Find could not attend the meeting in April, so they changed the date to May.

Even with three years of preparation, we landed a meeting with Child Find on the last day school was in session in our district. We felt defeated before we even stepped foot into that meeting. We knew this was likely going to be a battle. We knew we needed to bring in additional support, so we asked a Colorado Hands & Voices advocate to attend our meeting as well as our Learning Specialist and therapists from his previous program, and administration from our school of choice. We prepped with Hands & Voices in writing our parent statement, and they informed us about what to expect in the meeting. We gathered more information about our son's needs where we had holes, and we entered the meeting well-prepared.

The meeting was nothing short of brutal. Our district observed our son with completely different eyes. Parent choice for us was a school where communications needs would be met and he would have 100 percent communication access 100 percent of the time using American Sign Language (ASL) and English. We also needed a school where he would have support services for his mobility, feeding, respiratory and vision needs. Communication was a major factor where our team and the district did not see eye to eye. In a meeting that was set for an hour and a half, we took two hours, and only finished the evaluation and initial eligibility. Placement was far from being discussed. Consensus was not even in sight. Since it was the very last day of school, we had to

Team Bishop (Kyle, Katie, Lincoln and Marti)

schedule another meeting for August. The wait through the summer was unbearable. So many questions filled our heads and we wondered and worried how this would all turn out. We did not just sit idly through the summer. We had more assessments done, gathered data and documentation, wrote comparison notes of the different schools we had visited and how they could or could not service his needs, and we made sure that we knew our parent and child rights in special education to be ready for the fall.

We received an email at the end of summer stating that the district scheduled our meeting two days before the start of the new school year. Knowing that the meeting had been set in the eleventh hour caused undue stress to our family, but we had no choice in the matter. Again, the sense of defeat set in, but we would not let it remain. We were prepared. We had a lot of fire in us to face whatever came our way and we had our people. We reached out to our team of advocates, educational team, therapists, family and friends. We continued to push through the obstacles and remembered our goal of getting our son the most appropriate placement that fit all of his needs.

As anticipated, the second meeting was no better than the first, but we were not going to back down. The district continued to place focus on our son's mobility and therapy needs and disregarded the needs around hearing and communicating. As we moved toward placement, the facilitator wrote all possible choices on the board and we discussed which needs could be met where. It came down to two schools, the school of choice that we wanted as parents, and the school the district preferred. Both schools were deemed appropriate for placement by the district. After three exhausting hours, endless disagreements and tears, the district finally agreed to honor our parent choice. I nearly fell out of my chair and could barely remember what anyone said after parent choice was granted. It was a tough road to get to the end result, but worth all of the hard work we put forth in advance to stand up for what we knew was the best placement for our son.

We are so thrilled to be part of the charter school family and grateful for Hands & Voices and the endless support and encouragement they have given our family throughout this process. We are grateful for the educational team and therapists from Kid Street, and for the team at Rocky Mountain Deaf School for making the transition a smooth one. Our son is thriving in his new educational environment.

Preparation is so valuable. Always remember that you know your child best. Trust in that. Stand up for what your child needs. Find your people. One of our biggest assets throughout this process was the people we had in place. We reached out for advocates by our side who knew more about the process and law than we did. They were able to fill in the gaps where we did not know what to ask or look for. They helped us prepare. We reached out to professionals who have worked with our son. They gave us documentation and information about our son's growth, where he currently stood, and provided goals for continued growth. We connected with our family and friends who gave us solid support at so many levels. Let your passion carry you through, but keep your eyes on the end goal: our child's success.

While learning to be an advocate for your child in the IEP arena can seem intimidating, frustrating, and never-ending at times, I like to think of it as just another skill that I may have never had the opportunity to learn if I had not been blessed with such beautifully unique children.

Gwen Bryant

Learning to Advocate for the Unique Needs of My Son

By Yasmin Martinez

I had to point out to one provider that this was not a behavioral problem; this was a hard of hearing child, and I had to ask her to leave the meeting.

This has been a rollercoaster I never imagined I would be on.

The journey for my son and myself--being a single parent and with three other children who are hearing-- has been a huge life lesson of perseverance. My son, Daniel, was born able to hear, but he was a premature baby with many medical conditions.

At the age of five months, Daniel was hospitalized with respiratory syncy-

tial virus (RSV) and diagnosed with asthma. Shortly afterward, we started to deal with ear infection after ear infection along with high fevers. We gave every medicine prescribed, a process that was also required by our insurance company before they would consider any other treatment.

We spent many nights and months in the hospital in his first year of life. Daniel received therapy for motor skills and speech all while dealing with medical issues month in and month out. During all this time, I was never told he had any issues with his hearing and never suspected it. He had his tonsils and adenoids removed right before turning one. However, the ear infections continued. He had his first tubes placed at 18-months-old. Daniel continued to have ear infections almost every two months, and often the medication did not seem to work at all. When Daniel entered school, he had many hearing tests and none of the tests showed any signs of hearing issues. However, the medical issues continued and it seemed he was always on medication.

When Daniel was entering sixth grade, I received a letter from the school stating that he failed his hearing test and that I should take him to the doctor. At that time, Daniel was struggling in school. The doctor stated that Daniel had a lot of fluid in his ears and that the tubes were not doing their job.

It was then that I started noticing the impact of hearing loss in his daily life. Daniel turned up the television very loud and I had to nearly scream his name when in another room to get his attention. We had another surgery to have the fluid removed and to place a new set of tubes. At this time, I asked the school for help as Daniel was struggling in his classes and now he was dealing with some permanent hearing loss. The school team put Daniel through many assessments in order to see what services they would be able to get approved since he was not deaf, but rather hard of hearing. Daniel was able to pass sixth grade, and at the end of the year, they wrote a 504 plan for the following year.

"We Can't Serve Him Here"

When Daniel entered seventh grade, the boundaries for the district changed. Daniel would have to attend a brand-new school. I wanted to be proactive. I reached out to the principal that summer and asked if I could meet with him to discuss Daniel's 504 plan and make sure it would be in place for him from day one. When I sat down and started to explain to the principal about the 504 Plan written by the other middle school in the same district, (where he had actually served as an assistant principal) he said, "I don't think we will be able to accommodate him here, as I don't know how to get him those services."

I was confused. Why couldn't they follow the same plan? The principal followed up with an email, repeating that they couldn't accommodate Daniel. He told me to look into one of the other schools in the district for deaf students. I did just that and went through interviews and meetings. I was told a few days before school started that Daniel did not qualify for the deaf education program. Their advice? Keep him at his current school.

Not knowing what else to do, I enrolled him in the school and continued to ask for help from the principal, and then turned to the district office. There, I had a meeting with the district coordinator, who sent me back to the school after speaking to the principal. She shared some directions as to how to provide access services for Daniel. They put Daniel in regular classes but we were still having many meetings to discuss and develop supports and accommodations for the IEP he finally had. By the time the team had what was needed, we were in the third quarter of the school year.

Daniel worked very hard his last semester. He was struggling, and that seemed to be his new normal. He was confused and exhausted, trying to understand everyday instructions and communication at school. He wasn't able to hear clearly and continued to have ear infections. While he was trying to be a "normal" kid, Daniel started to shy away from friends that spring. However, he still loved sports. He was running cross country and playing basketball and travel baseball. As he entered his eighth-grade year, the ear infections continued, and Daniel was also trying to deal with his now progressive hearing loss. We started the year again with meetings to make sure accommodations would start from day one: preferential seating, extended time, get his visual attention before speaking, copies of teacher notes, an extra set of books for home, and more. For eighth grade, I decided to email each teacher at the beginning of the school year and ask them if they could please provide the services stated in his IEP. Most teachers responded and some provided regular accommodations, but this began to slip as the year when on. I started to receive reports that Daniel was not listening or paying attention in class. Some of the teachers suggested that maybe he needed to talk to a behavioral counselor.

I dug deeper. The teachers said my son was not listening to them and that "he just does not respond when talked to and does not ask any questions." After another hearing test, we discovered his hearing had declined significantly from the summer before. This time, hearing aids were suggested. Once Daniel received his hearing aids, he struggled with trying to become used to the amount of noise he was hearing in the classroom, from shuffling papers to talking. The new noises were distracting for him. He had a hard time focusing. He also said that at certain times throughout the school day, he couldn't hear. Did his hearing fluctuate?

We learned that on those occasions, which Daniel described as "hearing in a bubble", his tubing was clogged from ear drainage. I was always taking his hearing aids to get tubing replaced or sending them back to the manufacturer for repairs. Since his hearing had declined, the school wanted to try an FM system to help him. However, teachers would let the microphone rub on their clothes or the noise of the overhead fan would distract him, leading Daniel to take off his aids in the classroom.

I ended up spending a lot of time at the school from this year on. As his mother, I needed to be his voice, even though I did not have a clue about being hard of hearing. Making his communication needs clear when his hearing seemed to fluctuate and his hearing aids sometimes seemed ineffective, was difficult. Some of the staff at the school believed Daniel was ignoring what was being said or asked of him.

High school found Daniel struggling and failing some of his classes. The teachers in high school had no mercy and disregarded his IEP at times. I contacted the district office again and asked for their assistance, and this time a whole team of teachers and support staff along with special education coordinators joined the meeting. Some of the wording and accommodations were revised. We requested a note-taker, but were told that notes could not regularly be expected from high school teachers for any student. He proceeded with even fewer supports in high school, even though he was failing some classes.

As a sophomore, the school tried soundfield amplification vs. the FM that he had to carry to each class. It took too much of the teacher's time to set up, and the charge would not last through the day. The school had a lot of technical interference with the soundfield, and Daniel continued to have issues with his hearing aids from the infections. That year, we went back to the drawing board to figure out better access in the classroom. The district decided on teacher notes again until something else could be figured out. The hearing aids needed constant repairs, too. Later in the year, Daniel had surgery for perforated ear drums. Dealing with the ear infections and problems with accommodations, Daniel would come home tired and stressed from straining to hear all day.

Discovering CART

Daniel continued to push forward with his education and his love of sports. He loved being part of a team despite struggling to focus and to follow conversations with friends. He had a handful of friends that knew he was hard of hearing. As a junior, he focused on getting ready for college and playing baseball at the collegiate level. Unfortunately, Daniel battled H1N1 that year and he had to be out of school for a few weeks. Because he was already struggling with some of his classes, the time out while he was sick made it doubly hard for Daniel to stay on track.

At this point, I asked the school for additional help with accommodations. I received pushback from the team, stating that he already had an IEP and they were following it. Upon his return to school, I saw that his assignments did not include accommodations added for additional support. This time, I asked for a professional notetaker, and this was denied. They told me they could not afford to provide those services nor had they ever before been asked to do that.

"How many hard of hearing kids are there in this school?" I asked.

I learned there were three students, including Daniel. "Why can't you provide accommodations that these students are entitled to?"

I was told since the three students all had some useable hearing, they were expected to use their hearing aids to access information in their classes. They put the burden of communication access on the students.

At this point, I was very frustrated and concerned. I tried to research what I could do to help my child. I would monitor his grades and look at the work that was given to him. I knew Daniel was frustrated. He could get some teachers to give accommodations, but others did not. His homework did not make sense to him, he didn't understand what was being taught. I filed a complaint with the board of education because his accommodations were not being provided as written.

We met with an advocate who was deaf and she advised us to add real-time captioning (CART) services to Daniel's IEP. The school wanted to start a review process to see if Daniel would qualify and benefit from this type of service. Our deaf advocate explained how CART services would level the communication playing field and help Daniel to receive equal access. She assisted in getting people to attend our meetings in order to gain a better understanding of how to use CART in the classroom since they had never provided CART services before. We requested a trial for two weeks to see how this would help him. The IEP team tried to intimidate us, saying that Daniel could hear 95% of what was being said--which was his discrimination score on his audiogram. I felt I had to defend Daniel at every turn. The district always found something negative to say about CART and pointed out continually what an expensive option it was. They even said Daniel was lazy and he just wasn't paying attention and focusing. They just didn't want to spend money to provide equal access. I had to point out to one provider that this was not a behavioral problem; this was a hard of hearing child, and I had to ask her to leave one meeting.

After months of discussion, Daniel finally got his CART services for two classes. He chose his two hardest subjects, math and science.

While the school was highly ranked in the state, it wasn't working well for Daniel. Thinking that Daniel was going to fail a class, I signed him up for summer school and taught him at home to make sure he was going to pass. I finally filed a complaint. When the complaint was investigated, the ruling was in our favor. The school had neglected to provide his services in some of his classes. Daniel was able to work with a tutor to retake tests and complete the assignments. Daniel finished his junior year with decent grades.

In his Senior year, our battle continued for the CART services that had started just two weeks before the end of his junior year as a trial in two classes. We had to look at the data, which appeared to show that he wasn't using his CART services fully. They failed to note when Skype would not work due to dead zones in the building, or when he needed tech support. He had his trial during finals, where he would sign on for instructions, and there would be nothing for quite some time, so it appeared he wasn't using the service. That helped his cause greatly. The Department of Vocational Rehabilitation got involved, along with the college, and other advocates to help him complete his requirements for college.

Thankfully, Daniel found college a much more accessible place, using CART and a notetaker for all his classes. While he has had another two surgeries and issues with his hearing and infections, he continues to make great strides. Daniel started ASL in his second year of college, realizing that he may need it as his hearing continues to decline.

My experience with my son and his hearing journey has been a big challenge for me. I also made it my personal goal to make sure that my son has everything he needs to be able to have a chance and be successful. Many thanks to our advocate, our attorney, the Department of Vocational Rehabilitation, his support services at the college and the staff there, along with Hands & Voices. It takes a team to advocate. As a single mother with four kids, and late-identification of hearing loss, this journey required perseverance and the strength to never give up. Parents, continue to learn about and advocate for what your child needs. Your child does not fit in a preconceived box. There is no obstacle too big

Plan to tackle one obstacle at a time, celebrate successes no matter how big or small, and never give up! See your child as a graduate starting in the bassinet. Seek support from other parents who have traveled this journey before you and have confidence in your ability to advocate for your child. You are their first teacher and you know them best.

Lisa Kovacs

Deaf/Hard of Hearing Plus Means So Much More

By Kristen Stratton

I have spent a lifetime trying to figure out where I fit in as a hard of hearing person in a hearing world. I grew up in a family with a strong history of hearing loss but without the richness of language or culture; that seemed reserved for only those who were truly "deaf." I didn't know "Deaf" as compared to "deaf". I didn't know about the world beyond mine which had a full and complete language and was as beautiful as it was intricate and complex. I didn't know anything, until I became the mother of a Deaf child.

By the time my third child came along, I felt seasoned in my parenting. I fed my kids organic foods, did Pinterest crafts, was a devoted stay-at-home parent, forgoing my plans to become a successful attorney. I threw all my energy and abilities into motherhood.

I knew our family carried a history of progressive sensorineural hearing loss. I was identified hard of hearing at the age of five. Despite the need for hearing aids, I did not use aids until age 15. I did not receive any accommodations or supports in school beyond the cursory seat at the front of the class. When my own children were born, I admit I was fearful they would be "like me." I vividly recall crying when my second child "failed" his hearing test at birth. He had a repeat test several weeks later and I remember telling my husband, "I don't want this for him."

When he passed that second test, I felt relieved. As far as I knew, having hearing loss was a deficit in every sense of the word: something that would hold him back and make life harder. I look back on that memory with all the knowledge I have now and have a lot of compassion for that young mom who didn't know how amazing her kids could be and how beautiful her world was going to become.

Life carried on. We took all our children to routine audiology visits just in case. Up until the time I was pregnant with my third child, the only one who had any hearing differences was me.

My third child's labor was routine, until it wasn't. My son was born struggling to breathe and had very low APGAR scores. Due to reasons unknown, reasons which I no longer stay up at night trying to figure out, our beautiful son was brain-injured. It took years of doctor visits and missed milestones and mis-diagnoses to finally learn my son had cerebral palsy and he was developmentally delayed. Later, he developed seizures which made his already complicated language and learning even more of a struggle. During the diagnosis process, we also learned he had a severe bilateral progressive sensorineural hearing loss. He was Deaf/Hard of hearing Plus (DHH+++++++). Honestly, the hearing loss was the least of my concerns. I was just trying to keep my kid alive!

I would like to mention how trauma from that birth changed me. Many years of my life were spent putting the shattered pieces of myself back together. While not all parents have a traumatic birth story, some of our experiences raising children with significant medical needs, creates its own brand of trauma. It becomes the lens, through which we view our world. Trauma is with us in our day to day lives. It permeates our relationships and our careers and irreparably changes us. The best thing I ever did was go to therapy. I also poured my heart into helping other women have good births and worked as a consumer advocate for maternal healthcare. While I still struggle, therapy, the love of my children and husband, and my work in advocacy saved me.

When my D/HH Plus baby was not quite two, we sent off blood work to a lab for further diagnostic study. Shortly after, we were told he had a fatal genetic disease. While attending hearing aid and earmold fitting appointments with our toddler, we were also communicating with a program director at the National Institute of Health. We were grieving, broken, and preparing to fly to Bethesda, Maryland to enroll our son in an experimental study to extend his life. He might only make it to 3-5 years of age. We couldn't plan on a long future full of language and dinner-time chats and college graduations.

Call it a miracle or a medical mistake but repeat lab work done months later and just a few weeks before our planned trip to Bethesda

was suddenly clear and we were told he did NOT have a fatal disease. More trauma...more life-altering information. I had quit my job to be home with my son. My husband was sobbing in the ice cream aisle at Walmart. We were talking about end-of-life planning for our child. I am certainly not ungrateful that he was not dying; but that was a hell of a ride.

Phew. Okay, so now what?

What are his educational needs?

Now we began to catch our breath long enough to figure out how we

were going to choose to support the language and educational needs of this child. I re-examined my own childhood and the struggles I faced being stuck between two worlds: not hearing, but not signing.

I decided that my son's needs were different. We were going to give him opportunities to succeed in all manners of communication. We chose to give him a community and an identity. We chose to learn American Sign Language. We also invited a Deaf mentor into our home and whenever our son's health would allow, we networked with the Deaf community.

It was intimidating. It still is. Even with my own hearing loss, I am still working on feeling worthy enough to use an interpreter (which, for the record, has helped me immensely). For my son, I don't feel the need to justify any of his access needs. He deserves access to the world and that's what we are trying to give him: a healthy marriage between being Deaf and having other special needs and being unapologetically himself.

In that journey, we have overcome many, many barriers to access within the medical, educational, and religious communities and within our own families. What we have been able to do with those traumatic experiences is share our wealth of knowledge. It was hard-fought, expensive, time-consuming and overwhelming. We have turned what might have broken us and turned it into something beautiful.

I am now working as a Special Education Advocate specializing in serving D/HH families. I completed my Juris Master's degree and am looking forward to qualifying for the California Bar after I complete an apprenticeship. That proclamation is now published, so I will have to follow through!

The most miraculous transformation hasn't been related to any one person, but rather the whole community of people who have the privilege to know our son. He is the embodiment of pure love. His smile, warmth, playfulness, perseverance and fierce drive to be independent despite all that he must deal with, is truly awesome.

Some people use the term Deaf Plus to describe a child or individual who possesses Deafness as well as other diagnoses. While that is not a preferred term among some members of the Deaf and hard of hearing communities, I have chosen to use it for its metaphorical power. The "plus" represents all the many people we have added to our lives who enrich my son's journey by so generously sharing their language, love, time and energy. The plus also represents what a blessing he is to our family and how much value he has added and forced us to grow as people. The term Deaf Plus in our home represents not what special needs have taken away from a would-have-been neurotypical child; it is a statement which reminds us all how much we gained with our third sweet miracle baby. I couldn't be more proud to be his mama.

Ambitious Goals for Every Child

Although the goals for each child may differ, the Endrew F. Supreme Court decision concludes that "... every child should have the chance to meet challenging objectives." The IDEA demands more than some educational benefit. Rather, the IDEA requires "an educational program reasonably calculated to enable a child to make progress appropriate in light of the child's circumstances."

A new definition of educational benefit from the Supreme Court's decision in the Endrew vs. Douglas County School District 2017 case.

Learning to Advocate in Early Intervention

By Andrea Stambaugh

My son Axel was born with congenital cytomegalovirus (CMV). CMV is a common and preventable virus that is normally harmless to the general population. However, if you contract the virus while pregnant it can pass through the placenta and have severe effects on the unborn baby. Yet, only nine percent of women have heard of the virus. One of the many things that this still relatively unknown virus can cause is hearing

loss. In fact, CMV is the leading cause of non-genetic hearing loss. Axel has many subsequent diagnoses due to CMV. Some of these include a bilateral profound sensorineural hearing loss, spastic quadriplegic cerebral palsy, global developmental and fine motor delay. He is also nonverbal. I was told in the NICU that my son would be severely developmentally delayed for the rest of his life. When we came home from the NICU, we started to make decisions and set goals to begin therapy. With so many unknowns, I wished I had a crystal ball to predict the future. I had no idea what Axel would or wouldn't be able to do.

We began receiving developmental hearing therapy (DHT) through early intervention, during which the therapist would sign to Axel and work with my husband, family members and me to learn signs. When Axel received his first cochlear implant around 6 months old, we enrolled in auditory-verbal therapy (AVT) as well as speech therapy. When we first started, the AVT was working on oral communication, the speech therapist was working on communication with an augmentative communication device, and we still had the DHT working on sign with Axel. At an Individual Family Service

Plan (IFSP) meeting during this time, we were asked to narrow our communication choice to one method per the team's request. It was my decision to continue the therapies the way we had been, working on the three communication methods and exposing Axel to all of them. My main concern was that there may be different times in Axel's life where he might need a different communication option. I knew that receptively he was very smart. You could tell by the way he would look up at you that he understood what you were saying to him. It was just a matter of figuring out how to help him get his message out. I also felt as though it was important to allow him to choose the method that was easiest for him. At one point, there was some argument from some of the therapists working with Axel that I should not expect him to hear or see communication in one way and expect him to be expressive in another language. I went with my gut and just decided to model language to Axel in any way that I could. Sometimes in sign language, some modeling with his communication device, and oral communication. We continued to work with several different therapists on each communication method. I had no idea what the future would hold for Axel, but I wanted to give him all the communication options so he would be able to choose the one that worked best for him.

How Do Three Communication Modes Work Together?

Now that Axel is three years old and early intervention is behind him, he attends a deaf and hard of hearing preschool program in the district. He still receives speech therapy and AVT while we continue to focus on his oral communication, sign language, and the communication device. While he is still mostly nonverbal and has little use of his hands, I recently captured the sweetest video of him. His communication device is positioned in front of him, but slightly out of reach, which is not typically how AAC is used. Due to Axel's limited fine motor skills, his messages can be unclear, so we wanted to make sure that when he accessed the switches, it was intentional. He activates a blue switch to scan through the options, and once he hears the word he wants to say, he hits a red switch, and that word is spoken in a different voice. When I went back and watched the video again, I realized that he chooses the word "bubbles" but then he takes his hand off the switches and signs the word "no." He then returns to the switches to get to the word he actually meant to choose which was "blocks." I was thrilled to see him combining different communication tools together to successfully get his message across. He understands when people use sign language and oral communication to talk to him and even though he cannot respond using his actual voice, he will respond using a combination of his communication device and some signs. Depending on how he is feeling and how his cerebral palsy is treating him on any particular day, he may also do better if he is asked a yes or no question and he is able to respond by shaking his head no or nodding yes.

I always have pushed total communication for Axel. For three years, we have had so many therapies. My theory was that I would give Axel access to all the tools and he could choose the ones that gave him the most success. While at times I questioned my theory, my mom gut told me to stick with it. When I see these moments of successful communication seamlessly through multiple modalities my heart explodes. All I ever wanted was a way for Axel to express himself. I can't wait to hear all the things Axel has to say. It's been so rewarding to watch him grow.

Axel's signed version of "mama".

Everyone knows what he means!

Every decision you make, remember you are doing what you believe is best for your child. There will always be people who judge you and your decisions but there are way more people supporting you. You got this.

Celesta Bowers

The World is Our Classroom!

By Elizabeth Kalis-McGuire and Pamela McGuire

We are not regular moms. We are homeschooling moms. We are a family of two Deaf moms with a KODA (kid of a deaf adult) daughter and a Deaf son. Some people view homeschooling as limiting; we have discovered there are endless opportunities with a child-led education also known as: the unschooling/homeschooling journey. We've been very fortunate that we've gotten so much support from our families and our friends as well as our district regarding our homeschooling journey. Every year, we are required to be in compliance with our state/county homeschooling regulations. We do connect with our coordinator twice a year for an annual portfolio review ensuring that we are on the track and are abiding the state/county laws.

Our advocacy challenges are a bit different than inside of a traditional classroom. The utmost priority is to ensure that there is communication and language access in the home--this access is the foundation of the endless learning opportunities. In our household, American Sign Language (ASL) is our primary language. Our children's education is mostly based on hands-on experience fostering life-long learning. Yes, we are in school now 24/7 & 365 days a year. Our goal as parents is to guide and provide continuous loving so our kids can discover and nurture their passion in learning. Our homeschool approach is organic. Natural learning is primary.

We always make sure that there are reasonable accommodations available for our tours/visits throughout the country at various museums; national parks; zoos and so much more. For instance, we arranged an American Sign Language (ASL) interpreter for 11 of us (a group of homeschoolers & parents) attending Turkey Hill at Lancaster, PA. We conducted the "triple scoop experience" which included the admissions to turkey hill experience; the taste lab; and tea discovery – we had an ASL interpreter on-site. On another occasion, when my children enrolled in the CPR/First Aid class through Frederick Community College--they were able to provide an interpreter. For our trips to places such as the Alcatraz Island in San Francisco, CA – we had an ASL version of the cell house audio tour on an individual hand-held digital device. We had a similar experience at the 9/11 Memorial & Museum in New York City, NY. Both of them were amazing! Last but not least, our specular exotic experience at the Zoological Wildlife Foundation in Miami, FL, they were not able to arrange an interpreter but we worked closely with them and they accommodated us to come in during the least busy time of the day and week. They were able to set up a private tour for us along with our encounter bookings.

Advocacy takes teamwork and it's all about attitude towards how we approach those issues and make the best out of the situation.

Make Learning FUN

We believe learning should be FUN. Learning is something that we do together; from each other and from others. It takes a team effort to make this possible. It's also important for children to learn how to work independently, as well. This may be a bit tricky, but it takes all of us combined to make it work--just like a life skill we use in our daily lives. Homeschooling is not one size fits all. It takes commitment; dedication; one pours your heart into this 24/7 as you watch your children grow and blossom every day; and learning more about yourself. On multiple occasions, our children are our teachers!

Homeschooling has been such an enriching experience jumping into this journey as we homeschooled our children for 10+ epic years. Our advice for others who are considering homeschooling:

Life is short, embrace every moment you have. Be one of a kind. Be unique. We are born to stand out!

Here's a quote worth sharing: "Play is the highest form of research" as said by Albert Einstein. As the years passed, my children have soared and pleasantly surprised us with how much they enjoy reading more than 50 books per year! They are also avid entrepreneurs. They enjoy subjects like linguistics, history, photography, filming, and editing; alsosports and outside activities such as biking, volleyball, snorkeling, basketball, yoga, snowboarding, travel, outdoor adventures and more.

In addition, to keep up with current events and technology, YouTube is a great tool. Most of the videos are captioned (although not always accurately). After watching a video on YouTube, the content inspires discussions; we gain perspective; potential knowledge; discover new things and so forth.

If possible, we know it is important to provide deaf/hard of hearing children and their families and indeed all homeschoolers, whenever able, the opportunity to travel. Explore the world, near and far. This is one of the greatest hands-on learning you can possibly ever contribute. Travel is the ultimate education.

"

Developing a strong community around
your child's education is the best
thing that you could do for them. Join
organizations...become invested in every
aspect of your child's journey.

Gregory Facey

Learn Your Child's Rights

By Beth Donofrio

When I was little, I always thought about what I wanted to be when I grew up. One of the strongest desires I had was to be a mom. Thankfully, I was blessed with five children. All have had their struggles and successes in life growing up. Let me tell you about my daughter Aubrey... my beautiful, independent, strong-willed, intelligent daughter who also happens to be deaf. I've never been a fan of "labels" and one of the scariest labels I had to deal with when raising my kids was labeling my daughter as "deaf".

My mom, who I respected greatly, was a special education teacher. I always went to her for advice on life and with parenting. While we were just hanging out at home one weekend, our dog had jumped up and barked at something and my mother happened to notice that

Aubrey did not turn and look. For the rest of the weekend, unbeknownst to me, she was doing these little tests to see what Aubrey could hear. That Sunday before she left to go home, she brought up her concerns about Aubrey's hearing to me. I was a little shocked and thought she was crazy! Aubrey seemed to hear everything fine! She wasn't my first child; she was my second, so I should know these things, right? I even might have been a little defensive, but my mother (being my mother), was persuasive and convinced me to call Aubrey's pediatrician and make an appointment to have her hearing checked.

Luckily, I had a really great pediatrician. She got me in quickly and listened to my concerns, she listened to what my mom had told me and she very bluntly told me she wasn't able to tell me if Aubrey could hear okay or not. I honestly didn't think it was going to be that big of a deal. I thought they were going to tell me that maybe she had fluid in her ears from a cold and she wasn't hearing 100% but she was going to be okay. They performed a medical examination to make sure all parts of her ears were anatomically correct, which they were. They shuttled me into another room where there was somebody called an audiologist who was going to do some testing. At this point I was feeling pretty good since everything with her ears looked fine. In retrospect, I should have been upset because there was no fluid or anything wrong that would affect her hearing. The audiologist completed testing and brought me into another room to give me the results. He calmly told me that he felt my daughter had a severe to profound hearing loss and that I needed to schedule an auditory brainstem test (ABR). I think pretty much everything they told me after that I didn't hear because I was in shock. I walked out dazed and with a phone number to call the hospital for scheduling more tests. I don't even remember driving home. I just remember tears streaming down my cheeks and me wondering what this all meant for my beautiful little six-month-old daughter.

I waited for my husband to get home from work. I sat there holding my daughter rocking her and crying, thinking about what this could possibly mean and what might be ahead for her in her life. I remember crying for a couple of days. I remember calling my mom and crying to her. I remember my husband trying to be as strong for me as he could but I know this was just as scary for him.

We went to the hospital and we did this "very scary test" called an auditory brainstem response test or ABR. It sounded awful, like they were going to open up her brain! Actually, the test was not scary at all. It was very benign. She went to sleep, they put electrodes on her, they administered the clicks and the beeps and we all waited anxiously to see if her brain received or "heard" those sounds. I held out hope that this was all just a big mistake and she could hear and everything was fine. When I saw them walk back in the room with solemn faces, I knew this wasn't a dream and felt it quickly turning into a nightmare. They told me that my daughter had a bilateral sensorineural hearing loss and that she needed to get hearing aids right away. One of my first questions was, "Will she be able to talk?" They told me the one thing every parent doesn't want to hear: "We don't know what the future holds for her."

We walked out of the hospital that day with that devastating news. I looked down at my daughter as we left and there was one thing I knew for sure.... she was still the same beautiful, smart, strong willed, funny baby she was when we walked in the door.

Those were the days before the internet. While we have the internet to consult today, sometimes a glut of information is not much better than no resources at all.

One valuable resource that happened for me: a local organization connected me to another family that had a child much older than my daughter with hearing loss. The mom was kind enough to listen to the hundreds of questions that poured out of my mouth that day. I finally felt like there was somebody that knew what I was going through! Parent-to-parent support is so important on this journey.

As time went on, I learned about local resources, found out about a free sign language class at a local church, and was connected to the disability resource center in our county. I was blessed to be connected to a deaf woman who provided resources and support--she was an outreach person who connected with families who had deaf kids. Probably the best thing that happened to my daughter was me meeting and becoming very close friends with this mentor. She was the first deaf person I actually met and got to know--she was a mentor, role model, and guide all in one. She had a son almost the same age as my daughter and we just hit it off from the start. My mentor showed me all that my daughter could be: happy, educated, successful, married, a mom. To me, she had everything that I hoped all my kids would have one day. Aubrey's deafness didn't seem to loom over me as much when I saw all that my mentor had accomplished. She gave me hope. My attitude immediately changed. I became determined to not let Aubrey be defined by her deafness.

One area of importance I need to touch on: the importance of advocating for your child in an educational setting. The reason why I know things went so well for Aubrey was because I had spent hours learning about my daughter's rights in the educational system. I made sure to show the school district I knew the law and what her educational rights were. There were a few times when we requested certain things for her in the classroom and at first were met with resistance, but when I referenced the law and her rights, we came to an agreement.

Here is one example of an advocacy situation we faced:

My daughter spent her first few years of school at a co-op deaf program. By 2nd grade, she wanted to go back to her home school district. I explained to the school district that she would need an interpreter in the classroom with her for full access. Our district didn't think she needed one and refused to provide one. We placed her in the mainstreamed classroom in her home school without an interpreter and it ended up being a disaster for her. I fought once again and told the school district she needed a full-time sign language interpreter--and this time, they agreed. We had to stand strong to show them what her needs were and remind the IEP team they had an obligation to provide it for her. I can't stress enough how important it is to know what your children's educational rights are and how to advocate for them. Get a book, take a class, talk to other parents, explore the Hands & Voices resources, and learn about it. This is important! The first step begins with you.

I'm not going to go through every high and every low of this journey, but I will tell you this: never, ever underestimate your kids and their potential! Do not ever tell them they can't accomplish something that they put their mind to--we never know what they are capable of until they try. Time and time again, Aubrey has completely blown me away with things she's done in her life--things that I initially assumed she couldn't do because she was deaf. She never let her hearing loss hold her back. If she wanted something, she went for it. I was amazed at her perseverance, dedication, and hard work. She did well in school, she was a High School varsity cheerleader, she played softball and volleyball in high school. She was popular, she had lots of friends, and for the most part besides some typical teen angst, had a great childhood growing up. She went to college, she graduated and she has an amazing career. She has a wonderful boyfriend along with their two cats, and she's very content with her life.

Those times when maybe her or I felt her deafness was a roadblock to something, we figured it out, solved it, and made it work. I couldn't be prouder of who she is as a person and I'm so very lucky I get to be her mom! Yes, I didn't know what journey lay ahead for her when she was diagnosed, but looking back, I wouldn't have changed a thing. Aubrey is Aubrey, her deafness does not define her. Yes, it's a part of who she is and I would not have experienced the things I have, learned the things I have, met the amazing people I have, and lived this wonderful life without her being deaf.

Life may not be what you expect on this journey, but it can end up being just as wonderful and as amazing as you had hoped and dreamed it would be!

My biggest pieces of advice I can give:

- Never underestimate your kids.

- Learn as much as you can about what they want and what they need.

- Educate yourself, knowledge is power!

- You know your child best, be an advocate for them when they are little and teach them so they can grow up and be an advocate for themselves.

- Seek out support - socializing with other families who had deaf kids was a game changer for me.

- Meet and socialize with deaf adults as well! They are great role models.

- If one door closes, go open another, don't give up!

Most importantly, listen to your kids.... *really listen* to what they have to say. You can't give in to every whim, but if we truly listen to what they want and need, give them the tools to work hard to achieve it, they can tap into their full potential!

Sometimes, we just have to carry on through our storm without exactly knowing the way.

The support through the storm is what makes the difference.

Kodi Brandt-Ogle

Role-Playing Builds Success

By Sara Kennedy

I vividly remember moderating a panel of teens and twenty-something students at a large conference, who were all deaf/hard of hearing. My daughter was standing at the podium, taking her turn telling her story about advocacy and the transition from high school.

Unlike the other four students, Maddie had not answered my emailed questions sent weeks beforehand to help the panelists prepare (and help me be a good moderator), so I truly had no idea what she might say next. This was not unusual for our relationship!

Her educational course had gone amazingly well once we got connected to services after her late-identification. Her midwife, our

family doctor, and I had all missed any issues with hearing at birth. She was our third child, and since her next older sibling's first words finally tumbled out in a paragraph at age two, I had not let myself worry about her lack of language until just after she turned one.

Focusing on the Positives

She had a lot going on in her favor. While we couldn't do anything about her late-identification or her profound hearing loss (severe to profound at birth and later progressing at age 4 and age 7), we took to heart that parent involvement was critical. We did our best to speed up our learning curve by reading everything we could and asking our professional team from early intervention to preschool to elementary and onward all the questions we had as they came to us. We attended every conference and met other parents as often as we could. Her siblings went to sign classes and attended school at her center-based program. They often had instruction about Deaf Culture and how to include their sister in family life.

Strategies We Kept in Focus

We knew that language, reading and writing were going to be key, possibly more important than speech. We placed a higher priority on comprehension and incidental language than perfectly clear speech, but as it turned out, she seemed internally wired to listen and speak well despite her audiogram. When we learned about Theory of Mind, that concept lit a fire under us to give her greater access to abstract ideas and her own problem-solving. More and more, we would answer her questions with "What will happen if you do this? What about that?" to get her thinking. We created lots of role-plays during those years about how to approach people and used characters in stories to talk about the perspectives of others. She kept a list of idioms starting in 3rd grade until she could recognize them. She looked them up or got the meaning from context as she was able. We kept her hearing technology up-to-date and retrieved it from trampoline pits and movie theaters seats (a magnet had become stuck to the metal when she fell asleep at a movie not long after receiving an implant). We let her have down-time with equipment, too, but did our best to encourage her to use her equipment especially while she was catching up. We turned captions on early and sold the idea to her older siblings that they would be better readers (they were). For any parent, those early years are a slog.

Another strategy was preparing all year long for IEP meetings. Maddie said in her speech to that conference group that we always brought "stacks of books and information" to her IEP meetings. People were scared. (I doubt it.)

- We wanted to bring ideas for new accommodations and goals or strategies to help her succeed, not just engage in a discussion of "problems" without proposing solutions.

- We took to heart the "make a year's progress in a year's time", so looked ahead to what a freshman should be able to do versus an 8th grader, etc.

- We gave her every opportunity to learn about her rights under the ADA for the future.

- We kept reading and researching. We learned that deaf students can have difficulty developing a formal "voice" in their written work, and that was true in Maddie's case. We asked for help from the general education teachers.

- When it became clear that speech services were going to be discontinued in 8th grade, we asked for an Independent Educational Evaluation (IEE) of all her language skills so that we would know her reading level and any deficits in pragmatic language. The triennial IEP had not offered that and the current therapist was not well-versed in deaf education, so that was agreed to easily and was a help in goal production for the rest of high school.

Because we chatted with teachers, interpreters and educational audiologists all year long, we rarely needed the "stack of books", but it made me feel more prepared! While it was embarrassing to her in middle and high school, she learned to realize that her parents' role - and eventually her own role as an equal part of the IEP team was critical to her success.

In 8th grade there came a more difficult learning moment for all of us. Maddie started to express concerns about her interpreter's conduct at the end of 7th grade and the beginning of 8th grade. We knew that it wasn't a best practice to have a sole interpreter with her since leaving the center-based deaf program in 3rd grade, but there were upsides to that decision and no real other option, either. We touched base every year with each other to see how this was going, but I had left Maddie out of that discussion. Lesson number one. Since I knew the interpreter so well by now, I first brushed off her concerns as "teenager-hood". I wish I had responded sooner, and I wish Maddie had been able to make it clear to me what was happening. The interpreter correcting other students' behavior and making comments about Maddie as a student was becoming a reason that kids avoided her and was injuring their interpreter-student relationship.

Once I realized what was happening, I joined my daughter in sharing her concerns with the interpreter, and then the principal and the interpreter, and finally the special education department, who finally agreed that managing behavior of classmates was not the role of the educational interpreter per the state guidelines. It was too late in the school year to save their relationship. I am still sad to this day that someone we knew for so many years no longer wants to have any relationship with either of us over the finer points of that difficult discussion. I have no doubt Maddie was difficult to work with during her maturing perspective as a teen about what was once acceptable in elementary but no longer in middle or high school, and how difficult that must have been for both of them to navigate without other support.

Coming into her own Advocacy Role

That brings us to the last big goal... self-advocacy. While we focused on this from toddlerhood through middle school, ALL her IEP goals from 9th grade forward focused on self-advocacy, and the accommodations geared toward giving her equal access compared to peers as much as we and the district, and now Maddie herself, could agree. She had goals around seeking clarification/asking questions of her teachers a certain number of times each week in order to pre-empt communication miscues. She agreed to a trial of a captioning system to see if she would benefit from more access. (She ended up not using it in high school but did like CART and notetaking in college.)

Encouraging her to enroll in a vocational class kept her from dropping out as a junior when she didn't see the academic classes as relevant. She eventually settled on entering a nursing program, first focusing on becoming a certified nursing assistant at the school's recommendation.

My husband and I were "hands off" coaches and consultants at this point. She moved out, which helped her independence. Maddie eventually faced a big test of her advocacy skills and her belief in her own abilities. Unbeknownst to us, the director of her nursing program told her she couldn't possibly pass the stethoscope portion of the testing with her hearing loss. Maddie knew that the disabilities office and the vocational rehabilitation department should be able to help her with access to specialized equipment. They were very slow to respond. She didn't want to ask her parents until she felt she had no other options. Three days before the director had asked her to drop the class by the drop deadline, Maddie finally told us how the director came daily to class to urge her to drop the course and change her major. She was not sure the two offices even knew what to do to help even if she could get an appointment in time. I knew right away there were two modified stethoscopes she could use, and found both and ordered them (luckily, they could be returned if needed). The night they came, Maddie practiced with her dad and me several times but was not confident she had it right. The next day, she told her instructor she was ready to practice with her new equipment. Her instructor wanted to test her out on it. Maddie wasn't so sure; remembering that she only got two tries to pass the test within a very small margin of error. The instructor assured her that this was just practice. The other students crowded around. When Maddie took the blood pressure of a classmate, and it was the same result that the instructor got when listening with a connection of her own, she passed Maddie on the first try. The other students said that Maddie's equipment also gave them better hearing and thus better results. "For the first time, being deaf gave me the coolest equipment that worked the best in class, and everyone else wanted one," she said to me at the end of that day, elated.

I think about how many students would have just dropped out under all that pressure. No wonder the numbers of Deaf graduates dwindle in post-secondary programs.

She also faced significant barriers getting the accommodations she needed to sit for the state licensure exam, but this success inspired her to deal with the many emails and delays with getting an interpreter and the stethoscope to be accepted in testing. She continues to face some discrimination at work, particularly from co-workers who refuse to understand that a person might speak well but not hear well in noise and are otherwise fully capable. One thing she has learned and learned well... she is a hard worker who deserves a chance to show what she can do and have the accommodations she needs to make communication successful for any team lucky enough to have her fully included. When another attendee listening to the teen panel at the conference texted me "You did it!" I knew that it was not just me, but the many professionals who had worked hard with Maddie and with us as her parents, and Maddie herself who learned to place a high value on her dreams and her inclusion. She made this pinnacle moment happen. Your child can have pinnacle moments, too.

ADA, IDEA, IEP, 504, related services, accommodations, placement, audiology, language services, and speech therapy...

Feeling overwhelmed?

Nobody ever said raising a Deaf or Hard of Hearing child would be easy.

In fact, we can all agree it can be a challenge with stressful days, including some days where you might feel hopeless or lost.

One thing I've learned as a parent of a Deaf son is that I am my son's only voice.

Nobody will care about our children's success as much as we parents will.

Educate yourself, know your options, make well-informed decisions, and never take no for an answer.

Advocate for your child's right to reach their fullest potential.

Yiesell Rayon

Learning to Present Myself

By Tony Decha-Umphai

I was born in Nashville, Tennessee. I was born hearing, so I acquired speech at an earlier age. At the age of six, my hearing began to drop and my parents took me to an audiologist for a hearing test. After failing some of the hearing tests, I began wearing over-the-ear hearing aids through elementary, middle, and high school. I went to elementary school from kindergarten to 6th grade near Vanderbilt University. During that time, I was surrounded by hearing friends (including my hearing family). I had a chance to experience mainstream society. I was enrolled in special education classes and needed some tutoring to catch up with school work. While I struggled, it wasn't always perfect but I managed to pass all courses.

I went to middle school and high school from 7th to 12th grade in Bangkok, Thailand at an international English-speaking school. It was a private school where uniforms were required. Again, I was put into mainstream education without access to captions or interpreters, so I relied on classmates and their notes to help me get by.

I advocated for myself by sitting in front of the class and looking for a classmate who would share notes with me. Back in 7th grade, there was a bully who wouldn't stop picking on me. One day it ended in an altercation--a physical fight--but nothing too brutal. The next day, he shook my hand and apologized and from that point, there was no more bullying. I think I grew popular in high school because of a group of girls who really enjoyed talking to me. I didn't realize the extent of it until others nominated me for being most liked, most musically talented or most attractive, etc. I got voted "most attractive" from all the girls in the same grade. I was pretty surprised by that!

By 12th grade, my hearing loss became profound. I continued with hearing aids and struggled throughout the rest of high school.

There was one teacher who I called a "hardhead". She wasn't open-minded about my disability and gave me a hard time about it. I had to advocate for myself. I asked her to speak slowly and face me when she was talking to the whole class and to have someone take notes for me as I didn't clearly understand her 100% of the time. Back then, the school didn't have real-time captioning, nor did I know anything else to suggest. I didn't know sign language and the school didn't have interpreters.

Then came college where I went back to Nashville and studied at MTSU with a concentration in a pre-architecture major. I completed two years there, and then transferred to the University of Tennessee Knoxville with a major in architecture. While at UT Knoxville, I didn't realize I had access services until they provided CART for me while taking classes. From that point, I received the best education to date, being able to learn and absorb more knowledge through CART. I spent five years at UT Knoxville. Another turning point there was deciding to take off my hearing aids at times during class to see if I

could concentrate better. At times, wearing hearing aids mentally wore me down between the auditory and visual messages, and it often difficult to concentrate on certain subjects.

What my parents did right in helping me to gain confidence was giving me independence in socializing with my hearing peers. My twin brother and my mom were always there for me during any tough times. My mom also focused on teaching me to be likeable. Surprisingly, because I was likeable, people seemed to respect me more.

After graduating, I returned to Nashville to work for my first architecture firm who specialized in retail and commercial architecture. For two years, that went well, until the economic downturn. I and other staff were laid off during the 2009 recession. I didn't find work for about a year and a half. Eventually, I found two side jobs at Lipscomb University, working as a stock clerk and food prep worker. The stock clerk job was physically demanding, lifting heavy stuff most of the shift, but I did that just fine and it was nice to get away from the white-collar job for a bit. Still, I was determined after a year there to find a job in my major. I found an architecture company specializing in healthcare who hired me.

While at first it was a struggle helping the employees to learn to communicate with me and what I needed, I managed and got through it just fine. I am still working with them more than eight years later.

What I believe worked for me was to be straightforward with colleagues about my profound hearing loss/deafness and what I needed. Everyone understood it once explained, and we kept the nature of our work professional in that matter. As long as you let the other person know what you understand or can't understand and what you need them to do, it helps them to accommodate you and your needs. With the growth of technology, things are changing and becoming more accessible. So, living in this mainstream society, life has been going smoother since I've learned to be more open about my deafness.

Rather than dwelling on where the student is performing, we are now promoting the 1:1 rule. The rule states that every student should be making at least one year's growth in one year's time regardless of his or her performance level. One year's growth in one year's time, no less.

While the IDEA supports providing a basic floor of opportunity for students, the ADA addresses equal access.

In some cases, the ADA may provide a higher standard than the IDEA.

Cheryl Johnson, Hands & Voices Headquarters by Axel's Journey With CMV

The One Question to Ask at IEP Meetings

By Karen Putz

I attended my first IEP meeting as an "advocate" fresh out of college at my first job. The parents contacted me to help them convince the district to allow their child to attend a high school which had a program serving deaf students. I sat in the IEP meeting and passionately advocated for the parent's desired placement in the deaf program.

The answer was no. The child had to stay in the high school as a solitary deaf student with an interpreter. Seeing the sadness on that teen's face was devastating.

I left that meeting feeling defeated, confused, and... mad.

I was determined to never "lose" an IEP meeting again.

I ordered the book, *From Emotions to Advocacy, The Special Education Survival Guide* by Pam and Pete Wright. I shared that book with every parent I met. Over the years, families began contacting me through word of mouth and I attended IEP meetings when they became "stuck." Some meetings were 30 minutes. One meeting was five hours. Another took five meetings before the team came to an agreement.

In every IEP meeting, the goal is to level the communication playing field, no matter the hearing level of the student. 100% access.

During the five-hour IEP meeting, the team was going around and around the same issues. The district was fighting hard to keep the deaf student in their newly-formed special education classroom. The parents wanted the child to begin kindergarten in a school that had a specialized program for deaf and hard of hearing students in a communication method of their choice.

Finally, I asked a question that enabled us to move quicker to an agreement.

The question was simple:

"Is there any reason we cannot try _____?"

Insert the requested accommodation--then sit back and wait for the answer. Repeat the question until you get a "yes."

If the school district is balking because of funding, they cannot legally share that as a reason. By answering this question, the district has to legally explain why they cannot try the accommodation.

In one situation, I was helping a family advocate for real-time captioning in the classroom for a high school student. The student was doing "just fine" in the classroom according to the teachers and the itinerant teacher. His grades were mostly As and Bs--but he was achieving this by studying hard every night. He was stressed out in class each day, trying hard to understand everything being said. The school offered to provide a swivel-chair in every classroom so that the student could quickly turn around and lip read the classmates (I kid you not!).

By this point in the meeting, the mom was crying. The school district simply would not budge on the real-time captioning.

Then I asked the question:

"Is there any reason we cannot try the real time captioning for two weeks?"

The room went silent. Everyone turned to look at the special education director. I asked the question again.

Deep down, we knew the real reason was the cost--that's why the district was reluctant. Legally, they could not state this as a reason.

This time, the answer was "Yes, let's try it". They had run out of real reasons why it could not be done.

The student came home the first day of using captions and told his mom, "I had no idea how much I was missing in the classroom until I saw the captions."

He graduated with straight As.

Today, that student is an attorney with his own private practice.

The next time you attend an IEP meeting that's stalled, ask the question, "Is there any reason we cannot try _____." Then repeat the question until you get to the "yes."

To wrap up, remember this: Every child is unique. The bottom line for advocacy is to create a world which includes 100% access, and allows *your* child to thrive.

In Conclusion

As you have read through each story, you can see and feel the invisible thread of advocacy and determination to address the individualized needs of each student/child. These stories were shared to give you hope, and to empower you to never give up, and to always have the courage to create the next chapter of this book – your story, and your child's success.

Appendix

To learn more about educational advocacy, visit our website at www. handsandvoices.org/astra.

Look for the book: Educational Advocacy for Students who are Deaf or Hard of hearing, the Hands & Voices Guidebook on our website products.

Contact us directly to find parent-to-parent support in your area. We are parents with deaf/hard of hearing children, too!

More articles can be found on our website and through our newspaper and social media, like this one on the related service of Parent Counseling and Training, something available to all students on IEPs.

Parent Counseling and Training

By Sara Kennedy and Cheryl Johnson, Hands & Voices HQ

When parents and children leave the family-focused plans of Part C services behind as a child turns three-years-old, the focus of the services, goals and accommodations change. Families often feel less influential in determining the various components of their child's individual educational program (IEP). However, there are many important references to parent involvement as members of the IEP team and the IDEA continues to place an emphasis on families and family education. One additional reference that seems to be underutilized in some school districts can be a source for individualized education for parents. The description of this support is included as part of the Related Services section, known as *Parent Counseling and Training*.

What does *Parent Counseling and Training* mean? *Taken from the Individuals with Disabilities s Education Act, Sec. 300.34 (c)*:

> *(8)(i) Parent counseling and training means assisting parents in understanding the special needs of their child;*
>
> *(ii) Providing parents with information about child development; and*
>
> *(iii) Helping parents to acquire the necessary skills that will allow them to support the implementation of their child's IEP or IFSP.*

In addition, several other references mention parent training in the Related Services section. Under audiology, the definition of Audiology includes

> *(15)(v) Counseling and guidance of children, parents, and teachers regarding hearing loss;*

Psychological services include:

> *(10)(v) Planning and managing a program of psychological services, including psychological counseling for children and parents;*

Social work services include:

> *(14)(ii) Group and individual counseling with the child and family;*
>
> *(iii) Working in partnership with parents and others on those problems in a child's living situation (home, school, and community) that affect the child's adjustment in school;*
>
> *(15)(v) Counseling and guidance of parents, children, and teachers regarding speech and language impairments.*

In each state's IEP form, a section should identify the supports parents need to understand their child's development or acquire skills to support the implementation of their child's IEP. For our deaf and hard-of-hearing children, parent counseling and training might support language, learning ASL, communication, reading and literacy skills, safety skills, understanding technology or accessing community supports.

Parent Counseling and Training may be a key support parents are missing to support a child's achievement.

What Parents Hope School Staff Do and Say at IEPs

Remind yourself that this is a "lopsided" process for parents and students and do what you can to prepare and welcome us. (We might come into the meeting room without any of the eval results or forms, we may have no idea what to expect, and we feel like we're interrupting if the team is all present and chatting already.)

- Celebrate our child's strengths and use their interests in planning.

- Please remember my child is more than an audiogram or test result.

- Invite team members to listen to a hearing simulation or through a hearing aid as an education regularly. Equipment does not fix access or processing.

- Ask us/our child what we see as programming strengths/issues/ solutions.

- Promote shared problem-solving and decision-making with parents. student, and outside experts.

- If you promise something, please help implement it or get back to me. Keep us informed.

- Help us through being accountable for implementation of the plan. (I thought somebody else was doing that.)

- We know our child will miss information in a busy classroom or on testing even with (imperfect) technology, supports and services. Please take accommodations seriously. (Visualize a ramp for wheelchairs!)

- Take our concerns about school safety seriously. How will our child be alerted? Please practice in real time: i.e. don't make sure students who are deaf/hh are in the classroom vs. the bathroom or hallway, or avoid the drill altogether).

- Support emerging advocacy even if it looks like defiance. My child has to develop agency for a lifetime ahead.

- Assume until proven otherwise that first issues/behaviors relate to the student not hearing, seeing, or processing well.

Ask:

- How can we create a more deaf/hh-friendly classroom environment?

- How can we level the playing field for a deaf/hh student socially? (For example, in the lunchroom)

- How can we create listening breaks for eyes and ears to address listening fatigue?

- For a child receiving an interpreted education: The interpreter is present to provide access for all.

Remember:

- The interpreter is not in charge of education or behavior, the teacher is.

- Avoid referring to the interpreter as "Johnny's interpreter" – use our interpreter or the classroom interpreter.

- Avoid saying ASL or sign dependent; refer to ASL as a primary language.

By Sara Kennedy, Hands & Voices, with Mandi Darr, Colorado Department of Education Deaf Mentor Program, the Colorado Hands & Voices Staff, Guide By Your Side Program, and the Colorado Hands & Voices community.

10 Mistakes Parents of D/HH Kids Make in Preparing for their I.E.P

1. Didn't insist on a member of the IEP team who has specific expertise on deafness or hearing loss - allow the meeting to progress even if all required IEP team members aren't there.

2. Didn't ask for assessments/draft IEPs in advance of the meeting - don't understand how to read an audiogram, language assessments etc.

3. Let your emotions rule the day.

4. Didn't give school advanced notice of special or new requests. If you're pulling a kid out of placement, didn't give the school a 10-day advance notice.

5. Lose focus on what this process is really about - your child (not you, not the program, not the budget).

6. Stay quiet because you feel intimidated - and you're the one who sits down in the kid-sized chair at the table. You're afraid to ask the hard questions.

7. Don't really have a grasp on the implications of your child's hearing loss in the "real world"/educational setting.

8. Haven't prioritized your child's goals/accommodations from your perspective before the meeting.

9. Don't have a clue what IDEA really says - so you don't know whether the IEP provides a FAPE (Free, Appropriate Public Education)

10. Haven't created allies on your team before the meeting. Think that you and the IEP team can plan out your child's whole plan for the next year in an hour and a half meeting.

© Hands & Voices